Heavenly Praise for
Diary of a Modern-Day Goddess

"Cynthia Daddona is a very funny lady. She got me in touch with my inner goddess, who turned out to be an old woman named Maude Frickert. I was so taken by her book on enlightenment, I leave the lights on twenty-four hours a day."

—JONATHAN WINTERS
COMEDIAN

"Cynthia Daddona has a truly divine sense of humor—but what else would you expect from a modern-day goddess?"

—DOUG ADRIANSON
LOS ANGELES TIMES

"Humor and enlightenment should always go together. And they do—delightfully, with angels chorusing and chakras aligning—in Cynthia's new book."

—JENNIFER LOUDEN
AUTHOR, THE WOMAN'S COMFORT BOOK
AND THE COMFORT QUEEN'S GUIDE TO LIFE

"Cynthia Daddona helps us lighten up about everyday life with laughter and wisdom that is healing to the soul."

—BEVERLY KATHERINE KIRKHART
INSPIRATIONAL SPEAKER AND PUBLICIST,
CHICKEN SOUP FOR THE SURVIVING SOUL

"This book is bestseller material! I howled with laughter while reading *Diary of a Modern-Day Goddess*. Cynthia is a gifted writer and talented woman who knows how to share lovable truths and good common sense about a woman's true spiritual journey."

—MARIA DEL REY
GRAMMY-NOMINATED MUSIC PRODUCER

"Cynthia takes life's lemons and turns them into soothing citrus face masks, lemon incense and lemon chiffon pies. Her book will align your attitude and Feng Shui your spirit."

—RUSCHA ROBBINS
NOVELIST AND SANTA BARBARA HUMOR SOCIETY MEMBER

"Her humor mixed with very deep understanding is a metaphor of how to live. I plan to buy a copy for myself, my daughter, my stepdaughter and my granddaughter."

—LIZ RAY
AGE 70

"With her incomparable wit and wisdom, Cynthia demystifies a new paradigm of women today and brings honor to the intuitive spirit in every woman."

—MAGI MYGGEN
FENG SHUI CONSULTANT AND OWNER, INTUIT-DESIGN

"Cynthia Daddona is a real-life modern-day goddess. She has learned how to balance the stress of an active life with the need for inner peace. Luckily for us, she's written down the key to her success in this delightful, lighthearted book."

—SALLY FRANZ
AUTHOR, THE BABY BOOMER'S GUIDE
TO MENOPAUSE AND MONSTER LIES (XLIBRIS.COM)

"Cynthia Daddona is the funniest goddess I know—living or dead."

—IAN BERNARD
PRODUCER, WRITER, COMPOSER—"LAUGH IN"

"I loved this book. When I read Diary of a Modern-Day Goddess, I laughed and I cried, and sometimes both at the same time. Cynthia has hit the nail on the head with the realization that to have a better life you must first become a better person."

—JILLIAN MOON
PHYSICAL THERAPIST

"I loved this book so much I couldn't put it down. Cynthia is inspiring and uplifting while giving you applications on how to be a modern-day goddess who handles life with grace and humor. I can't wait for her next project!"

—JENNIFER ROBERTSON
HAIRSTYLIST AND THE QUEEN OF COLOR

"I felt inspired, encouraged, informed, entertained and uplifted reading *Diary of a Modern-Day Goddess*. Cynthia delightfully teaches that spirituality can be lived with laughter, intelligence, elegance and style. I loved this book so much I took it to bed and read it all once."

—ANNETTE GUIONNET
EXPRESSIVE ARTS THERAPIST

"Cynthia's humor is a beautiful tool in the never-ending quest for inner wisdom. It is also a reminder that laughter is vital to every goddess."

—MARIA HARAMIS
OWNER, SUNFLOWER SOAPS

"I like the lighthearted enthusiasm that Cynthia shows us as a way to live and bring forth the goddess energy."

—BARBARA "RAMA" SELTZER
REIKI MASTER, AGE 72

"As a male struggling toward consciousness himself, I can only hope there will be more goddesses like Cynthia to greet me when I get there."

—DEAN OPPERMAN
AWARD-WINNING COMEDY WRITER

"As an everyday kind of guy, I don't get to meet a lot of goddesses, and the only other time I've been 'enlightened' was when I accidentally shocked myself with a screwdriver and a live socket during one of those pesky home repair projects. Now, my favorite goddess, Cynthia Daddona, has shown me how to become enlightened without smoke coming out of my ears. She is a funny, talented writer, and she has made a believer out of me."

—ERNIE WITHAM
HUMOR COLUMNIST, MONTECITO JOURNAL
CONTRIBUTING WRITER, CHICKEN SOUP FOR THE GOLFER'S SOUL

"Buy this book for the woman in your life so she will feel like a goddess and you can get the TV remote back!"

—KABIR
A GODDESS APPRECIATOR

"Buy this book so Cynthia will be happy. And, if you're a single man and she's not married yet, call her."

—CYNTHIA'S ITALIAN MOTHER

Diary of a
Modern-Day
Goddess

Cynthia Daddona

Health Communications, Inc.
Deerfield Beach, Florida

www.hci-online.com

Library of Congress Cataloging-in-Publication Data is on file with the
Library of Congress

©2000 Cynthia Daddona

ISBN 1-55874-825-3

Publisher: Health Communications, Inc.
          3201 S.W. 15th Street
          Deerfield Beach, FL 33442-8190

Cover design by Lisa Camp
Inside book design by Lawna Patterson Oldfield

With all my heart, I dedicate this book to:

The divine mother of us all.
We are so blessed to have you in our lives.

My mother, grandmothers and
women of all generations who weren't
given permission or taught how to feel
like goddesses by totally nurturing
their inner-selves.

And to:

All the magnificent goddesses
around the world.

May this book invite you to
experience the divine nectar of your
joyful, feminine, spiritual self. And may you
be blessed by grace and laughter as you
explore the lighter side
of your soul.

Contents

PART III: MODERN-DAY GODDESS LOVE

PART IV: MODERN-DAY GODDESS EXPLORATIONS

PART V: APPLY MODERN-DAY GODDESS KNOWLEDGE TO YOUR LIFE

Acknowledgments

*C*he creative process has often been compared to giving birth, which isn't always easy. From the loving moment of conception to the intense labor of delivery, to the joy of the first time you hold it in your hands, I have been blessed with many wonderful people who have contributed to my life and this book. And, I would like to express a special heavenly thanks to the following souls:

All the talented and supportive goddesses at Health Communications, Inc., who believed in this book the moment they saw it. Thank you for your belief and enthusiasm about my baby.

The Editorial/Delivery Room Goddesses—Christine Belleris, for editing and nurturing me with grace, humor and compassion. Allison Janse for her professionalism, wit and can-do attitude. You are both a writer's dream come true.

The Art Department Goddesses—art director Larissa Hise, book designer Lisa Camp and the entire art department for creating a divine cover and book.

The Publicity Goddesses—Kim Weiss, Kimberley Denney and Maria Konicki for announcing the birth of my baby to the world.

All the Nursery-Room Goddesses who cared for my baby in their own special way after it was born: Book Signing Goddess Randee Feldman, Marketing Goddess Kelly Maragni, Sales Goddesses Irena Xanthos, Jane Barone and Lori Golden, Internet Goddess Elisabeth Sullivan, Audio Goddess Judy Perry and the Permissions Goddess Teri Peluso. Thank you for your support and enthusiasm

And, the Peaceful Warriors amongst the goddesses. HCI president Peter Vegso, vice-president Tom Sand and sales manager Terry Burke. As well as the entire staff at HCI, thank you for your professionalism in making my first book a dream experience to remember.

Linda Collison for taking such divine goddess photos of me for my book cover. You really captured my essence.

Graphic artist Lynda Rae, for the inside graphic she created by listening to my ideas and brilliantly making me appear in a clamshell.

Will Nix, my entertainment attorney, for believing in me and my vision, even more than I believed in myself when I first walked into your office five years ago. Thanks for always being there for me with your expert advice, guidance and enthusiasm.

The Santa Barbara Humor Society members for the comedy camaraderie. Thanks for the countless hours we've spent together humoring, listening and advising one another on what is, what might be and what could be funny.

Sally Franz, a friend, comedy colleague and visionary sister. The synchronicity of us meeting again in California was a heavenly blessing. The journey would not have been as much fun without you. Thanks for your support.

Ruscha Robbins, a friend and great "Brit wit" that keeps me laughing.

My favorite funny men: Ian Bernard, thank you for teaching me the craft of how to seriously write humor.

Ernie Witham, for your friendship and gentle witticisms— you make the world a better place with your humor.

Dean Opperman, for your hilarious accounts of man attempting to triumph over adversity. Your humor is better than a case of sublingual vitamin B_{12}! You are an inspiration to me.

And to the rest of The Santa Barbara Humor Society members, for their comments and support.

Janet Arena—thanks for your friendship and for guiding me to a place of meditation where I could open my heart and heal my soul.

Annette Guionnet-Geis—for your creative way of looking at the world, your nurturing and our healing beach-talk walks.

Magi Myggen—for your visions, intuitive Feng Shui and interior design tips.

Jillian Moon—for being the "Florence Nightingale" physical therapist who became a good friend as you twisted my wrist back into shape.

Judy Babcock, a personal well-being coach extraordinaire who humored and coached me through the final stages of writing and editing my book.

My cousin Jennifer Monin for the friendship and post-book retreat.

Maria del Rey, thanks for sharing with me what it means to be a woman pursuing her God-given talents. Your music, divine wisdom and beauty are a blessing to the world.

Jennifer Robertson, a talented hair stylist and philosopher. Thanks for lifting my spirits and giving me fabulous hair cuts so I can have more good goddess hair days than bad.

And all my other beautiful goddess girlfriends, who over the years have provided me with a circle of friendship. You have been a great source of support, laughter, love and comfort. Sonja van Mastrigt; my wise elder goddesses—Barbara "Rama" Seltzer, and Liz Ray, Robin Oriel, Kelly "M" and Leena Dillingham, Patricia D'Orio and Jenna Hardesty.

My parents for bringing me into this world. I wouldn't be here without you.

My mother who inspired me to tell funny stories, laugh and make a great lasagna. Thank you for all your love, the delicious meals and the countless hours you spent working for the family.

My father who told me at a young age, I could be whatever I wanted to be in life. Thank you for your love and the endless stream of positive thinking books you supplied me with in college.

My brother Carl and his wife Leslie, thank you for your love, never-ending support and encouragement to go after my dreams.

My stepdad Sam for the jokes and family boating trips. My stepmom Donna and half-sister Nicole for the family meals and laughter.

My brother Anthony and his wife Lynne, for the great e-mails and support.

My Italian grandparents. Thank you for showing everyone what Italian living was all about with your music, dancing, singing, stories and extra servings of love, hugs and mouth-watering food. I hope you are enjoying life in heaven—We miss you!

All my Italian relatives on the east and west coasts—for your love, sense of humor and for making the holidays so delicious. Special thanks to cousins Vicki Zenobio, Mike, Terry and Denise Dobain for being there when I graduated college and was optimistically looking for my first low entry-high paying job in the entertainment industry. And to cousins Marianne, Thom, Kent and Kristin Miner for your love, hospitality and the good meals.

Dan, who provided me with a vehicle for change.

My writing instructors—screenwriter Jon O'Brien, and author/journalist Martie Sterling—for giving me the knowledge of my craft and the inspiration that I could get paid to write. Gail and Gary Provost, for providing me with my first writers workshop retreat. We miss you, Gary. I'm sure you are in heaven, inspiring other souls to write.

My English teacher, Mrs. Stelmach, for helping me clean up my poor Italian grammar mistakes in tenth grade.

Kabir, for being one of the few men to read an advance copy of my book and liking it.

Simon D'Arcy, for showing up at the right time with your prayers and physical therapy follow-through assistance.

Tom Cunneff, for your inspiration and career advice.

Ken Miller, for your financial wisdom and wit.

Gail Kearns, a wizardess of words, for reading my writing under deadline.

To Jim Buckley, publisher of the *Montecito Journal*, for being the first to publish my writing in Santa Barbara.

Co-Ministers Eddy and Patty Edwards and the members of

Unity Church—for providing me with ongoing prayers and a place of community and inspiration.

Buddy Winston, the first man to ever call me the Goddess of En-Lighten-Up-Ment.

All the wonderful groups who have given me support, knowledge and encouragement to pursue my entrepreneurial goddess dreams. The great people at WEV, (Women Economic Ventures), Right Livelihood, LEADS; The Synergy Circle, The Artist's Way, NY Women in Film and TV, Women in Film (LA), Writer's Guild East-TIP, and the Santa Barbara Writer's Conference.

The Immaculate Heart Center for Spiritual Renewal, for providing me with a nurturing place to write and heal.

My well-being consultants, who over the years have provided me with many healings and insights into my life: Margaret Sweet, Leslie Moed, Luana Rubin and Stephen Barcia Bacon.

Oprah, for inspiring me to know that anything is possible for a woman.

God, for giving me the gifts of writing, speaking, humor and enthusiasm so I could make a difference in the world.

All my glorious goddess sisters who are out in the world living an authentic life. And everyone else who ever contributed to my life as a writer, you know who you are. A heartfelt thanks.

And last but not least, David Krueger, who met me as I was healing from a broken wrist. Your love, sense of humor, support, brilliance and computer savvy are a godsend. Thank you for walking the path with me, helping me to heal and inspiring me to love again. Because of you, my life has been "touched by an angel."

Introduction:
Be a Divine Beauty

Inside every woman is a beautiful goddess waiting to emerge. In the new millennium, a new female archetype is appearing. She is a modern-day goddess—a woman who accesses her inner spirit for guidance, courage, joy, inner peace and lightheartedness!

A modern-day goddess celebrates her feminine spirit. She listens to her intuition, communicates what she wants, discovers what she loves to do—and does it! She is guided by her higher power. Her very essence makes a difference in the world, whether it's by her smile, her creativity, laughter or the love she radiates. She is a woman living her authentic life.

I believe all women are born with the capacity to feel like a goddess until modern-day life and negative messages interfere. But the good news is the connection with one's divine power can be restored.

A woman can feel like a joyful goddess when she creates balance in her life by taking good care of herself, lightening up about life and spending time with her inner-self. This book is filled with the many experiences I sampled to create a more sacred, lighthearted and soulful life.

It is a spiritual journey that I found myself and many others traveling. A yearning to create a life away from the hectic lifestyle of "doing" and toward a more balanced and happier existence—toward "being."

Having been born in the early 1960s meant I graduated college during the time of the "superwoman era." Back then, women were filled with a lot of life options our mothers and grandmothers never had. The message that was driven into us was, don't let these opportunities go to waste—go out there and conquer the world. That will make you happy.

So that is what I did. I kicked into high warrioress mode. I sought out and landed creative, exciting but often stressful jobs in the movie, television and print journalism industry. I even performed stand-up comedy. These were major accomplishments for someone who came from an Italian-American family. I still remember being singled out in tenth-grade English for having poor grammar and a vocabulary that consisted of pasta, meatballs and "ciao"!

While my resume was packed with experience, the long hours and lack of nurturing time left me feeling burnt-out and disconnected from my feminine self.

Ironically, I once again shifted into the warrioress mode to conquer personal growth. I read so many self-help books I was exhausted from helping myself. I took the road less traveled, but it was gridlocked. I tried talking to my angels, but they called me back collect. I even tried to have a conversation with God on the Internet but his chat room *God.com* was full.

So what was wrong? I was back in the "doing" (masculine)

mode instead of the "being" (feminine) mode. In the *Heroine's Journey* by Maureen Murdock, she writes about how women injure their feminine nature when they try to be as "good as men." Murdock goes on to say that the task for the heroine is to become a "spiritual warrior . . . to learn the delicate art of balance and to have the patience for the slow, subtle integration of the feminine and masculine aspects of oneself."

So, that's what I did when life surprised me with a motorcycle accident as a wake-up call. It was an event that caused me to blend my male energy (the achiever warrior) with my female energy (the intuitive, feeling goddess).

I began to slow down, spend more time meditating, praying, laughing, nurturing myself and committing to fulfilling my dreams. In the end, I healed my wrist, my heart and my soul. I emerged a stronger, more balanced, feminine, light-hearted woman who will always listen to her intuition.

When a woman makes time for herself, even if it's only ten to twenty minutes a day, she will start to feel like the goddess she is meant to be. These deposits into a "self-nurturing fund" will keep her from becoming overdrawn when she is faced with modern-day life stresses.

And I know it works. Because now when I take the road less traveled, the traffic has cleared up. When I want to talk to my angels, they call direct, and the shares I bought in God.com split and made me prosperous.

While each person has his or her own path, I've included what I've learned from each experience in this book. In the end, I discovered the experiences that helped the most were the ones that always brought me back to myself.

This book was inspired by my own journal writings which

over the years have helped me heal my life, explore my creativity, and find my inner wisdom and higher power.

You can experience your creative expression and inner voice by keeping a journal nearby as you read each chapter and by jotting down any insights or reflections you may have about your life.

So, I dedicate this book of wit and wisdom to all the goddesses I have met who have shared their joys, laughter, challenges and wisdom with me, and to all of the future souls I look forward to meeting. Take the inspiration and laughs that work for you in this book, celebrate your divine beauty, and live the life you deserve!

Blessings,
Cynthia Daddona

Modern-Day Goddess Living

Can you remember a day of frustration and pain where it felt like a negative cloud was following you around? And no matter what you attempted to do, it didn't work out? A day when everything went wrong— from your bad hairstyle to the weather, from a flat tire to an argument with your loved one.

Can you also remember a perfect day or moment when everything seemed to flow and you felt like a goddess? Maybe you sealed the deal, shared a beautiful moment with your child, finished your book or spent a beautiful evening with your sweetheart. Chances are you were in touch with your feminine spirit and experiencing your goddess power!

While life will always be filled with ups and downs, a goddess can increase her chances of attracting great experiences into her life like a magnet. How? By aligning herself each morning with her goddess power and taking good care of her body, mind and spirit.

Here are two examples of a goddess and an un-goddess workday.

An Un-Goddess Day

Wake up at 7:45 A.M. Hit snooze alarm. Oversleep.

Look in mirror and criticize yourself for being late, having worry lines and your unruly hair. Skip breakfast.

Rush to work. Take freeway to get to work faster. Get stuck in mile-long traffic jam. Curse yourself and the drivers around you.

Sit in traffic listening to news on radio about crime, death, etc. Spill coffee as you squeal on two wheels into office parking garage. Hit boss's Mercedes as you wipe the stain off your skirt.

Arrive at work at 10:00 A.M., frustrated and scattered.

Apologize to boss for denting the fender. Smile as he tells you how you'll spend your paycheck for the next month. Plow through work on desk without break.

Take lunch break, but use it to run errands. Eat a McFatso sandwich in car while driving. Drip ketchup on skirt. Get two flat tires on the way back to work and think of it as punishment for eating unhealthy fast food. Call the auto club, which doesn't show up within the promised hour. Leave car on side of road. Take cab back to work.

Arrive at desk to see note from boss saying you need to redo the report—not good enough. Get stressed out and criticize yourself again—this time for not doing a good job.

Receive call from the auto club which has to tow car to tire dealership.

Need two new tires—total cost $149.99.

Work late to redo report. Eat stale peanut-butter crackers from office vending machine for dinner.

Return home exhausted. Play back answering machine with message from mother asking if you will ever get married. Watch TV and fall asleep on couch, aggravating sore back muscles. Grind teeth and dislodge molar crown. Relive the whole day again with a nightmare.

A Modern-Day Goddess Day

Wake up thirty minutes earlier than usual.

Flip on aromatherapy diffuser filled with "sacred place" oils.

Write three pages in journal to clear mind and focus on the day.

Focus on your vision board that has images cut out from magazines with what you would like to achieve. Look over your written goals. Review your balanced goddess life weekly to-do list that includes all areas of your life. Select items to focus on today. Pray and affirm that the "divine plan" of your life now manifests.

Begin your yin workout: Play soothing instrumental music to meditate to, and visualize a successful day. Do a goddess visualization where you ask your divine inner-goddess for guidance throughout the day.

Begin your yang workout: Stretch or dance to your favorite upbeat music. Go for a short walk in the neighborhood.

Eat healthy breakfast of fruit and grains or a fruit smoothie.

Dress in colorful outfit you love.

Drive to work while listening to books on tape or positive self-talk tape that you prerecorded with sayings like "Everything I do is a success. I can conquer all my challenges because I am the goddess of my universe."

Sip warm herbal tea in commuter spill-proof mug.

Arrive at work, relaxed and centered. Look at Dilbert calendar and chuckle.

Conquer work on desk, taking one to two five-minute deep-breathing breaks.

Take lunch break. Options include: Strolling in the park. Reading your favorite book. Working out at gym. Taking a yoga class. Having lunch with other upbeat goddesses. Eat, drink filtered water, laugh and be merry.

Still get flat tire on way back to work, but receive divine assistance from nice-looking coworker in convertible who happens to be driving by and stops to help you change tire. Acknowledge goddess synchronicity.

If you are single, return back to desk happy with a lunch date from coworker for tomorrow.

If you are in a relationship, return to your desk to find flowers with a beautiful card from your boyfriend or husband that says how much he loves you.

Listen to voicemail that has a message from your sweetheart that says: "Hello my goddess, I was just thinking about how special you are to me and how wonderful our life is together. I love you and can't wait to see you!" Walk to water cooler and laugh with coworker and talk about inspiring *Touched by an Angel* episode. Return to desk to see report with a note from boss saying *Nice job!* Get invited to company's yearly awards dinner. Finish rest of work by end of the day.

Leave work and go to dinner and fun cultural event with a great date, friend or your sweetheart. Tell your evening's companion how much you appreciate his or her company.

Return home. Listen to wonderful messages from friends and family. Read an inspirational book before falling asleep or watch Jay Leno's monologue for some funny jokes. Cuddle with your teddy bear, spoon with your sweetheart or nestle in your beloved's arms as you watch *Touched by an Angel* dressed in white. Fall asleep counting your blessings and looking forward to another goddess day. Enjoy a peaceful heavenly sleep.

Making Goddess Days a Reality

I've experienced both of these days above. But now the un-goddess days only happen a few times a year. By waking up thirty to sixty minutes earlier each day to practice my goddess nurturing techniques, using any commuting time or early morning time for positive learning, taking several five-minute deep-breathing breaks throughout the day, eating healthy and exercising, I've been able to create great goddess days on a consistent basis. My goddess days run smoother and save me time in the end because I spend a little prep time praying, meditating, planning and asking for guidance. Of course, depending on a modern-day goddess' lifestyle of being single, married or with children, retired, working in an office, running a corporation or her own business, the scheduling may vary.

I know many of you are saying, "Sure, that sounds great, but I don't have the time." My response is, if we have time to brush our teeth, then we should be able to make time for ourselves and some very much-needed goddess maintenance. As women, we can't afford not to take care of ourselves and nurture ourselves. If we don't, the results are stress, fatigue, disease, burnout, accidents, low energy and lack of joy about life. And if we end up at the doctor's office or sick in bed, that's a lot of time and money wasted that could have been invested in you.

So take good care of yourself, reclaim pieces of your hidden self, laugh every day, carve out time to take breaks and spend some quality time alone, even if it is only for ten minutes a day. Be deliciously nurturing to yourself—as much as you can stand. Because the rewards will be great and your inner-goddess will be filled with joy.

Inner-Wisdom Realization

You have the power within you to create a day that nurtures and empowers you.

PART I:

Go West,
Young Goddess

2

A Very Moving Goddess, Act I

Dear Diary:

It was years ago when I asked myself: Could a single, thirty-something, starving writer/stand-up comedienne/aspiring TV personality with a flicker of faith, an intuitive hunch and a wheat-gluten intolerance follow her dreams to become a success story? Yes, I now know it can be done. But what I didn't know then was that to have a better life, I would have to become a better person.

Today I asked myself, how do people get from where they are to where they want to be? For me, it's been faith, perseverance, courage and a good sense of humor.

So where do I begin? My journey toward creating a divine, beautiful life has been a great, big adventure. One filled with challenges, triumphs, tears, matters of the heart, blessings and a motorcycle accident that broke my wrist but luckily not my funny bone.

9

There is so much to say and so many lessons I've learned along the way to become a modern-day goddess—a woman in touch with her inner spirit, inner soul and inner laughter.

Now, when I look back, I can see how my dips into the divine provided me with a protection of grace, a strong inner-self and synchronicity of events that changed my life forever.

I know everyone has their own path, but here is my story that began when I was down and out in the ritzy town of Westport, Connecticut, hearing the whispers of my intuition that said Go West, Young Goddess!

It was a cold and windy winter day. The worst snowstorm the East Coast had seen in years had finally stopped. Several feet of snow were piled up outside my studio apartment. I was snowed in with a bad case of the northeastern winter blues.

I sat frozen in thought on my futon couch. What was I supposed to do with my life? My vision of inspiring and entertaining people as a television personality was being blocked at every turn. I had a degree in broadcast journalism, but I didn't fit into the standard TV news-reporting world. I tried working for a small ABC-affiliate news station in college, but I was too sensitive. Whenever I heard bad news, I cried afterwards. Each day I became more and more emotional. It got to a point where I started to cry over the good news, too. Then the news director finally took me aside and said perhaps I wasn't cut out for news. He was right, and I left the station the next week.

I laid down on the couch, thinking about my short-lived news-reporting career, and wondered if something was wrong with me. Spiraling down in thought, I recalled the twenty-four-year-old agent at a top New York talent agency who bluntly told me I was a nobody unless I had a published book or my own television show. Even when I created my own entertainment show on Connecticut cable and won an innovative cable award, it still wasn't enough. I remembered showing it to a top cable network in New York. "The production qualities are poor," said the executive. *What did he expect from a ten-year-old VHS camera I got from Goodwill?* I thought to myself.

"I had hoped you would see past my limited production budget of fifty dollars and recognize me as a new talent," I answered.

"Sorry, we don't work that way; you need to have an agent."

Westport, Connecticut is a wealthy, artistic seaside town. I was struggling to survive financially, in a place filled with heiresses, trust-fund kids, arts, entertainment moguls—and me.

I wasn't an heiress, and the only trust I had was trust in myself, but even that was running low. Through it all, I continued to work a variety of freelance jobs as a public relations consultant, a TV and print lifestyle journalist, humor writer and a stand-up comedienne. I followed screenwriter-director Nora Ephron's advice to take your material and keep moving it around to different mediums until someone buys it. I was juggling my multimedia talents, even though by then I would have preferred to be a successful multimedia maven.

I spent most of my time on the phone in Connecticut looking for work and setting up appointments in New York City. For the interviews, I put on my power suit and joined the briefcase brigade that commuted an hour by train to Manhattan. This routine yielded a few weeks of work and then nothing for a month.

In the city, I traveled all over by bus, cab and subway, clutching my bag full of headshots, resumes, demo tapes and a low-budget lunch of a banana. The meetings either resulted in intense hours of freelance work in writing, TV interviewing, producing—or rejections that said I was too something . . . too old, too young, too innovative, too conservative, too tall, too short. One day, I even thought about modeling and stopped off at a modeling agency. The five-foot tall receptionist stood defiant, taking one look at my petite five-foot, four-inch frame and announcing "They don't give appointments to anyone under five-feet, seven-inches tall." I felt as if I was having a flashback to when I was nine years old and was rejected from Disney World's Space Mountain because I was too short.

To stay alive in between the dry work spells, I took work as an office temp when it was available. At one point, I even waitressed and performed at a local comedy club. Overall, I did not feel like a modern-day goddess but more like a burnt-out woman.

The chill in the room brought me back to the present. I sat up and wrapped myself in a blanket. I lit a candle and contemplated a realization I had a week before at my Italian mother's house. I remembered standing in her warm kitchen, mulling over my unhappiness, while the garlic wafted through the air.

I watched her stir a huge pot of homemade tomato sauce and thought about our different views of success. Her idea of success was for me to be married, while my idea was for me to have a great career. Looking back, I can see they were both about external things and nothing about internal things like self-love, joy and happiness. As my mother lifted the wooden spoon of sauce for me to taste, as she had many times before, it was then I realized I had finally come to a place in my life where I had reached the spoon in the road.

The wind blew more snow against my window. I got up and made myself a cup of Tension Tamer tea. It didn't help. As I waited for the water to boil, I knew there had to be a better way to live, and my hunch said: "Go West, Young Maiden!"

I wanted to live in the land of sunshine and palm trees. The home of the creative, spiritual and beautiful people. A state that gave birth to Gidget, the Beach Boys and three essentials of California living—the convertible, Jacuzzi and Thigh Master.

I started chanting the word *California* for a double confirmation. I had recently been introduced to chanting on New Year Eve's when a spiritual girlfriend invited me to join her at an ashram. (My other options were to stay home and wallow in pity, commiserate with my single girlfriends or go to a party where people would drink themselves unconscious with alcohol. Going to an ashram sounded great!)

At the ashram, I learned that chanting and meditation opens the heart and helps you connect with your inner-self. So I asked my inner-self to confirm California. I continued to chant and visualize the words *California, Connecticut* in my head. Before long, the word *California* glowed, and I knew I had my answer.

Not having a lot of faith at this point in my life, I still wanted a triple confirmation. So I asked God what my life would be like if I stayed in Connecticut. I raised my eyes to the heavens and noticed a pine tree branch heavy with snow over my skylight. As I said, "Please God, show me the light!"—a squirrel jumped on the branch, the pile of snow fell with a thud and I was left sitting in total darkness. So much for the light. I looked up again at the snow and this time it seemed to have melted into the shape of California. Or perhaps I was imagining it. Nevertheless, I interpreted it all as a sign to leave Connecticut.

But how do you go about moving three thousand miles from a conservative Connecticut town to sunny California? I had the faith, some courage, but not much cash. I was afraid to take such a big risk. Then I remembered the saying: "Jump and the net will appear." Of course, that could also apply when the folks in the white coats come to get you.

I looked outside and noticed the wind had stopped. I slowly rose to get some fresh air to clear my head. I opened the door and took a broom to punch through the snow blocking my door. I stuck my nose into the cold air like a ground hog seeing if it was warm enough to venture out. It wasn't. I shut the door and sat down at my desk. "Okay, God," I reasoned. "I'm turning this over to you. If you want me to move to California, you will have to show me the way." Within moments, the phone rang. It was an online magazine editor. A few weeks ago, I had pitched a story idea involving an interview with Bette Midler for her new movie, *That Old Feeling*. The editor loved the idea and encouraged me to attend the press junket, where journalists from all over go to one hotel to interview the stars of the film. But, if I wanted to go I would have to take care of my own lodging and airfare. I said, "Yes!" Then I hung up the phone and danced around the room singing, "California, here I come!"

My mind raced. I grabbed my infrequent-flyer file from the cabinet that was covered with cobwebs from the lack of use. I called several airlines, and between my frequent-flyer mileage, bonus points from my credit card, and my willingness to ride in the cargo space with the Chihuahuas and poodles, I manifested a ticket to California. Another miracle had occurred.

But where would I stay? I had some Italian relatives in California, but none in the central area. I called my mom, who has always been resourceful, and she reminded me of a high school girlfriend who was now a model/actress in Los Angeles.

The next thing I knew, I was at my girlfriend's place in West Hollywood, adjacent to Beverly Hills. The following day, I sat in the Four Seasons hotel pressroom feeling fabulous. I was dressed in a light, lime-colored, spring suit, sitting with several other journalists as we interviewed the Divine Miss M. What joy! Her courage, wit and perseverance inspired me. I asked Bette what motivated her to keep going. "Why, the bills!" she answered with a laugh. "They come in, they need to be paid, and I say, 'Well, I guess I better put my high heels back on!'" I was having a great time and thought to myself, *This sure beats standing knee-deep in snow digging out my car.*

Okay, God had gotten me to California, but where was I going to live and how would I survive? I prayed and continued to ask my higher power about my destiny, plus everyone else here on the Earth plane. Asking is something I learned country to assist with the upcoming booksignings for Stephen's new book *King Con*. A rep was needed in New York. I told him my media experience and got the job.

I then returned to Connecticut and pulled off a successful book signing for Stephen Cannell with some great media bookings for him to be interviewed on shows in New York. I found Stephen to be a kind and encouraging man who succeeded as a writer despite his challenge of dyslexia. I felt if he could beat the odds through persistence and focusing on his talent, so could I. I was so inspired by him that I started working diligently on my book.

There were days I was certain about giving up my studio apartment and moving to California, while other days I was filled with doubt. Since I come from an Italian family with a long line of worriers, I was also fearful. What if I failed, what if I starved to death, what if I was allergic to palm trees? I reasoned I could always come back and live with my family in Connecticut—but the thought of being in my thirties and living with my parents made me even more determined to succeed.

To calm my fears I called a few people to ask for encouragement. I talked to my girlfriend in New York who had introduced me to chanting. She said: "I'll miss you. But remember the New Year's Eve message we heard at the ashram. 'Wake up to your inner courage and become steeped in divine contentment.' You are supposed to practice it all year." Her words hit me like a bolt of lighting. I had an "*aha* moment" when I realized everyone has courage inside them, and no matter where I lived, I would still have to figure out a way to find work while pursuing my dream. So why not do it in paradise?

I then recounted my blessings of a round-trip ticket, the story assignments and a place to stay in California to my younger brother Carl, who has always encouraged me. He said: "It's obvious your angels have been working overtime. Go for it."

My Italian mother was definitely sad to see me leave Connecticut. I was the oldest child and her only daughter. But since living in California had always been one of her dreams, too, she wished me well, put on her sunglasses and sundress and said, "See you soon!"

Next, I called the Arts Fellowship leader at Marble Collegiate Church in New York City, who had always enthusiastically cheered me on to pursue my dreams. What else would you expect from an advisor at a church founded by Norman Vincent Peale—the father of positive thinking. My advisor's advice summed it up: "When God is at the door knocking with the moving company, it's time to go!"

3

A Very Moving Goddess, Act II

Dear Diary:

I've come to the conclusion that some places seem better when you are only visiting them temporarily. Moving from conservative and cold-weather Connecticut to sunny, casual California really appealed to me. But it wasn't until I lived in West Hollywood that I realized I wasn't a city girl but a country girl who longed to be by the sea. (The nearest beach was twenty minutes away without traffic, but an hour and a half whenever I tried.) The glamour of West Hollywood soon faded. And from this experience, I learned the importance of a modern-day goddess finding an environment that soothes her soul and makes her heart sing. I am so glad I eventually found my special power place in Santa Barbara, California.

Whether a modern-day goddess feels her power in a brownstone in New York, a cottage by the sea or a tent in the mountains—that is up to each woman. But after talking to others, I've discovered certain spiritual power places are especially popular with goddesses, such as Sedona, Arizona; Sante Fe, New Mexico; Ojai, California; Boulder, Colorado; Hana, Maui, Kauai; Martha's Vineyard, Massachusetts; and, according to my mother, all of Italy.

I arrived in West Hollywood feeling like an immigrant stepping onto Ellis Island with a bag full of dreams, hopes and optimism. But luckily God had arranged for me to be in an apartment complex that felt like a resort. Each day, I wrote by the pool and marveled at the palm trees. It turned out I wasn't allergic to them after all.

I was in a very trendy section of West Hollywood, one block off Sunset Boulevard—a street lined with nightclubs, upscale clothing shops, huge billboards and rows of popular outdoor cafes where the beautiful people, celebrities, industry types and Europeans dined daily. West Hollywood was a high-stimulus area to people-watch and be seen.

But the excitement of being in sunny West Hollywood wore off as soon as I completed my journalist assignments and began looking for work.

My girlfriend, who owned the apartment, was away and I felt isolated. It was tough finding work, and within a month, I began to feel even more down than when I was in Connecticut.

Nevertheless, I was persistent in my search for jobs in the entertainment industry. First, I called an alum from my journalism school—the University of Florida. He was a smart, successful journalist who gave me a list of TV and film publicists to contact. Each morning, I mustered up my fearless goddess attitude and began to dial. Next, I began my asking and faxing campaign. For this, I would call, ask about work and then fax them my resume. Some days, I was a busy faxing goddess, and other times I was a post office goddess where I spent hours waiting in line to mail out demo tapes, writing samples and my spec sitcom script.

Determined, I also applied to be a host for a lifestyle television show in Los Angeles. I sent in my tape, only to be told I looked too young. I called back a few days later and asked the secretary to let the casting director know I had spent all weekend in the sun, so I now looked older. Still no appointment.

Another contact got me an audition to be a comic who would warm up the audiences before tapings of a new television show. A lot of comics were vying for this steady gig, and they eventually chose someone who had ten years of experience and a clown outfit.

One day in June, I saw an ad in the paper, not for a job, but to be a contestant on a new game show with a big cash prize. Again, the competition was stiff. I did well during the audition and got all the correct answers, but lost during the practice of showing *high-voltage* enthusiasm. In the end, they chose an opera singer who could yell louder and jump higher than me. What a blow to my self-esteem when I realized I couldn't even get work as a game-show contestant!

During this time I uncovered another harsh reality. Most of the entertainment industry goes on a summer hiatus. When I looked into applying for a sitcom writer's job I was told all the writers had been hired back in March. I felt defeated and even called a few restaurants for work. But I discovered there was a waiting list to be hired, and the manager was a producer, the hostess an actress and the busboy a director.

In only six weeks, I had suffered daily rejections, my first earthquake tremor, a heat wave and a major culture shock at a Coffee Tree. I felt I had hit bottom on a day when the temperature reached over 90 degrees. When I discovered the air conditioner in the apartment was broken, I attempted to find comfort in the local chic caffeine café.

Many coffee places are a microcosm of the local residents. On this day I sat inside admiring all the attractive men and women with perfect skin, blonde hair and ultra-white teeth. Many of the women had collagen lips and baseball breasts—you know, the ones as hard as baseballs and guaranteed to hit a home run. It was a stunning crowd, but I felt as if I were in the middle of a store called Plastic Parts R Us.

Because of the heat, most of the women wore itty-bitty camisole tops, micro-mini-skirts and short-shorts. This caused the men to pant so heavily I thought I might actually witness a silicon meltdown. I was also fascinated by the supertoned biceps many of the woman sported. I was curious what purpose they might have served. As I watched a pint-size petite female with toned biceps drive by in her convertible with the wind whipping through her hair, I realized they were needed to help the svelte blonde hold onto the steering wheel to prevent her from flying out of the car.

There was such an emphasis on outer beauty; I wondered how much time was spent on developing their inner beauty. It was then I realized I didn't belong in a city like West

Hollywood. And I felt I had made a big mistake in my move because I wanted to be by the sea. Instead, I got up and settled for an herbal tea.

While in line, I ran into Giselle Fernandez, who was then one of the hosts of the entertainment news show "Access Hollywood." I had met Giselle in New York when I worked backstage for the Grammies collecting interviews for CBS's international news feed. I said "Hi" and got up the courage to ask if "Access Hollywood" needed any interviewers, field producers or writers. She was kind and told me to give her a call at the office. I left with my spirits lifted.

I dropped off my demo tape at "Access Hollywood" in Burbank followed up with several calls, and a few weeks later I had a freelance job as a vacation relief field producer for the week before Labor Day. I was thrilled until the reality of the long hours set in. For those five days, I worked twelve-hour days, watched twenty hours of video footage, wrote scripts, drove all over LA gathering sound bites, and stayed up twenty-four hours to edit a piece that was to air the next day. By the time I was done, *I* was the one who needed the vacation relief. On my last day, I asked one of the top executives if there was any possibility of being considered for my dream job as a field correspondent. I told him I was a good interviewer and writer, then gave him my headshot and said: "This is what I look like without the dark circles, after I've had some sleep." He chuckled and thanked me for my help, but said there weren't any openings, since on-air talent at "Access Hollywood" rarely left.

So, I let go of the idea of working my way up from an entertainment field producer to reporter. It was Labor Day weekend, and I needed a break. I decided to visit a comedy colleague from back east, who coincidentally had moved to Santa Barbara the same day I moved to Los Angeles.

I drove ninety miles north of Los Angeles to Santa Barbara. When I drove into town, I felt at home. Santa Barbara is a peaceful place with feminine energy, majestic mountains, the beautiful ocean and clay-roofed Mediterranean homes. Some people call it God's country; I call it goddess country.

My girlfriend and I laughed a lot and explored the town. Over the weekend, we were invited to a local brunch and two Labor Day beach parties. At one of the parties, I learned about an upcoming Santa Barbara goddess festival and met people who would later provide a vehicle for change in my life.

After the weekend, I returned to Los Angeles renewed and with the idea I might move to Santa Barbara. But after a few days filled with more rejections, my hands began to shake with fear. So at a friend's suggestion, I went to see an acupuncturist to calm me down. My session consisted of ten or more needles inserted into various body parts. Surprisingly, it didn't hurt and it did help me relax, even if I looked like a pincushion. Afterward, I sat in the acupuncturist's office pouring out my troubles. When I finished he looked me in the eyes and said: "You need to meditate!" and handed me a schedule from a local meditation center. He was absolutely right. I had received another "aha moment" from the universe.

I attended the meditation center the very next night. I found great comfort and warmth there. The people were kind, centered and happy. They were focused inward and not outward like the West Hollywood coffee crowd. And the chanting and meditation began to provide me with serenity.

I also learned how all kinds of grace and assistance had

shown up in people's lives from quieting the mind, focusing on the inner-self and connecting with the divine.

One woman said the same thing could happen to me. She pointed me toward the temple and said: "Go in there and ask for divine assistance for everything you need. Everything!" So I did. I got down on my knees and asked for the divine plan of my life to manifest. But I said it would be nice if it also included a job, a car, a new place to live and, as long as I was asking, perhaps a husband?

I continued to meditate, and my life did change for the better. Within a month, I found a great inexpensive sublet with a kind woman who also attended the center in West L.A. (Only five minutes from the beach!) By now, it was September and people were focused on work again. Next I obtained a series of freelance jobs connected with books. First, I worked for three months lining up comediennes for a comedy book and met inspiring people like Sid Caesar, Carol Burnett and Norman Lear.

When that job ended, I worked two months on a media project for bestselling inspirational author Barbara De Angelis, and then as a public relations consultant on a project for two more bestselling inspirational authors, Gay and Kathlyn Hendricks, who happened to live in Santa Barbara. God was definitely showing me I should be involved in inspirational books.

When my sublet in West Los Angeles ended, my girlfriend in Santa Barbara and I decided to become housemates. We realized the synchronicity of us moving to California on the same day when we became humor-writing colleagues and champions of each other's dreams.

While I didn't obtain a husband in that short amount of a time, my last wish of a car was granted when I found a white '89 Mustang convertible for a few thousand dollars.

In Santa Barbara, I attended the goddess festival I learned about at the Labor Day beach party. It was a fascinating event, held at a beautiful music academy. There I met many wonderful women who later became my friends. I was amazed that the theme of the festival focused on women celebrating their feminine self. It was the same message I wrote about in my book. This confirmed, once again that I was on the right track.

From that festival, I was invited to attend a workshop for entrepreneurial women focusing on their right livelihood and becoming financially successful. When that group ended, I joined LEADS, a women's networking organization for women to provide business leads to one another. Our LEADS group consisted of twenty of the most nurturing, spiritual and entrepreneurial women I had ever met. We had members who ranged from an investment broker to a personal coach to a Feng Shui consultant. I guess you could say I was now a Santa Barbara networking goddess.

I continued my public relations consulting, wrote a column for the local newspaper, joined a writer's group and attended the Santa Barbara Writer's Conference, where I took workshops in screenplay and humor writing. I also worked as a journalist for the Santa Barbara film festival. Each week, I walked on the beach and meditated at the local center. Within six months, I felt a real sense of spiritual and creative community. And I knew I had made the right decision to move.

A year later, the Book Expo came to Los Angeles and I felt

I had to attend. At the event, I was once again the asking athlete. I took my book proposal and enthusiasm and went from booth to booth asking publishers if I could submit my work. It wasn't easy, but this time I had stronger faith in myself and lots of testimonials from women who loved my book.

Within a few months, I received several rejection letters that started with openings like: "You are a witty and talented writer . . ." and ended with "however, we only publish books with humor from famous people" (there goes that "you are a nobody" theme again) or "we don't think that people who want to be inspired also want to laugh" (my friends and I do!), and "your book has too much of you in it" (but it's a first-person diary-biography).

The night before my birthday, as I recounted my rejections, I felt a bit down. I had spent the last year working hard in a writer's group and had given my all to marketing this book. I didn't know what else to do except pray. That night I went to the local meditation center and gave thanks in prayer that the divine plan of my life manifests and said, "Hi God, it's me again. If you really want me to inspire people with this book, you've got to give me a publisher real soon. Okay?" I then turned it over to God, left the center and went to bed.

Letting go of what I wanted worked! The next day, I received a call offering me a publishing contract, which was one of the best birthday presents I ever received.

Now when I look back, I am glad I took the risk and listened to my intuition to move to the West Coast and to keep moving until I found my special power place. I feel so blessed to be living in Santa Barbara, California—a town of feminine spirit, the mountains, the beautiful ocean, populated with many gifted healers, artists, writers, inspiring men and goddesses. It is here I feel I've found my spiritual and creative community, or what Julia Cameron calls in her book, *The Artist's Way*: "my tribe."

The other day, I received a call from a girlfriend back east who described a snowstorm in progress between her sniffles from the flu. "I'd love to move to California, too. I just wish I had your courage to take risks." I smiled as I looked outside at the warm sunshine and heard the birds joyously singing.

"You do have the courage; every goddess does," I said. "It's a matter of having faith, trust, perseverance, the willingness to ask for help and take action. Or as Oprah said: 'The only courage you ever need is the courage to live your heart's desire.'" I also added: "Of course, I've learned a healthy savings account will help reduce the stress, so start saving now."

As I hung up the phone, I felt very much at peace with my life. Even though it was a rough journey moving from conservative Connecticut to trendy West Hollywood, the experience made me realize how a modern-day goddess can transform her entire life by listening to a hunch.

Inner-Wisdom Realization

You can make your dreams come true by having strong intention, asking your higher power for guidance and accessing your inner courage.

Modern-Day Goddess Contemplations

1. Do you have a hunch about your life that keeps coming into your mind?
2. What's preventing you from taking action?
3. Are you living in your spiritual power place? If not, can you visit or read about it? Or can you take action to create a special power place where you live now?
4. Is your work aligned with your life purpose?
5. Who can you ask for help in making your dreams come true?

What I Learned

Outer beauty is hollow without inner beauty.

External success is nothing without internal happiness.

Never give up on your dream.

Ask, Ask, Ask, Ask, Ask!

"Feel the fear and do it anyway," as author Susan Jeffers says.

Believe in yourself.

Find your tribe.

Like it says on the dollar bill, "In God We Trust."

Trust in God.

4

The Lucky Break

Dear Diary:

God has been so good to me by bringing me to Santa Barbara and giving me a happy life. But I didn't know what I was missing until he gave me a cosmic kick in the pants in the form of a true "lucky break."

I should have listened to my intuition," I thought as I woke up in the hospital in Santa Barbara wearing a full-length arm cast.

I wanted to take the car, but my freedom-loving, adventurous boyfriend wanted me to experience the joys of motorcycle riding. I gave in and became the loving, passenger girlfriend—a role I had played many times in the relationship.

I tried to remember what had happened next. I remember lying on the ground, being scared and praying to God, archangel Michael and my spiritual master to be with me and protect me. I remember a kind paramedic who told me funny jokes in the ambulance to keep me from thinking about my pain. He told me his name was Michael, and I thought, *Wow, an archangel with a sense of humor. How lucky I am.*

The door to my hospital room opened, and my rugged, adventurous man entered and sat in the chair next to my bed.

It had started about a year ago. I met him and entered into a relationship I thought would give me the things I wanted, like love, financial security, fun, adventure and travel. I got these things, but found they didn't make me happy. We had a relatively good relationship by some standards, but something just didn't feel right. The idea of marrying him was an ongoing discussion between my mind and my heart. I constantly asked myself whether it was fear of commitment or my intuition saying this was not the man for me. I prayed to God and asked for a sign, a way I would know if we were supposed to be together, if this was the path I was supposed to take in my life.

Meanwhile, a sharp pain in my wrist brought me back to the present. "Hello," I said to him softly, still a bit groggy from the painkillers.

He smiled. "I've got good news and bad news," he said. "The good news is that the bike is okay, and I got you a card. The bad news is that your wrist is shattered, and it needs reconstructive surgery. Oh, and by the way, I don't have any insurance on the bike or for the passengers."

I felt another sharp pain, but this time is wasn't just my wrist. I laid there and tried to process everything he had just told me. I was too tired to speak, so I closed my eyes. I felt him slip the card into my usable hand and kiss me on the cheek. When I woke up a little while later, I opened the envelope. In it was a get-well card with a photo of a motorcycle in a circle with a slash going through it. I shook my head, laughed, then cried.

I asked myself what was the meaning of all this. I decided to interpret this as God saying "No!" It was time to make a break. And since I hadn't been listening, God made the break for me. I'm just glad it wasn't my neck.

My answer was clear. Part of me smiled when I thought back to my prayers for a sign. I said "thank you" and made a mental note to myself: Next time I pray for a sign, *ask for gentler answers*.

From that day on, I've learned to listen to my intuition. I had plenty of time, considering I had two reconstructive wrist surgeries, three hundred hours of physical therapy and pins inserted and removed. Oh, and the adventurous man and I? We "broke" up.

In a love relationship, each partner has special gifts. Sometimes the gift—like the gift of adventure—is not the right gift for you, and therefore, this person is not the right partner.

Being laid up for almost a year after the reconstructive wrist surgeries which sapped my energy, pumped me up with anesthesia, antibiotics and upset an already-sensitive stomach, taught me to listen to my intuition and get my life back in balance. I did this by loving and nurturing myself in a way that I never did before. By having faith in myself, I've been able to pursue my creative dreams.

During that time, I could only type with two fingers and most of the time I barely had enough money for gas and food. I was turned down for disability as a "two-fingered" writer because I was self-employed and hadn't paid for the policy in advance. Through it all, my faith, meditation, courage, girlfriends—and, thanks to my archangel Michael, a sense of humor—kept me going.

Luckily for me, even though I had only been living in Santa Barbara, California, for five months, I had connected with the community through a woman's networking group, a meditation center, a writer's group, a Unity Church and a girlfriend from back east. It was humbling. I let go of any pride and spent several hours each week on the phone asking people for things: my groceries, rides to doctor's appointments and physical therapy, help with cooking and with almost everything else. Everyone was so kind, I felt blessed that God had sent me a team of angels.

It has been written that resilient people look for the lesson in a crisis and aren't afraid to ask for help. I will always remember the impact this accident had on my life. Once I learned I could rely on my inner-self and a higher power, I began to experience joy, courage, love and even laughter in the face of adversity. This resulted in a deeper commitment to loving and trusting my inner-self and to creating a more balanced lifestyle. It opened the door to the adventures and misadventures that have become this book.

I've learned to be more observant of the events and people around me, for they bring with them signs and answers. *The Celestine Prophecy* says "there are no coincidences," and I believe that; our angels and the universe, or God give us answers through many different means. It's our intuition that helps us recognize these answers.

Now as I continue to do my wrist strengthening exercises in hope that my joints will be able to handle the usage and pressure they once did, or when my wrist hurts from damp weather or I see the scar, I feel a tinge of sadness for the physical loss but it is mixed with gratitude that I am still alive after a motorcycle accident and a commitment to always listen to my higher power.

Now each time I recognize an answer to a question I have in my mind, I smile. I think of what it took for me to realize how wonderful it is to have "divine guidance"—and how, by being aware of it, I need less of a cosmic kick in the pants!

Through this cosmic-to-boot therapy, I found I have an avenue to the answers, and it is through me. In the end, this experience launched me into a journey that would change my life forever. When I look back at the motorcycle accident that cost me a year of my life but could have ruined my life, I choose to call it my lucky break.

Inner-Wisdom Realization

You don't have to wait until you have an accident, illness or a "cosmic kick in the pants" to nurture yourself and connect with your higher power. You can begin now.

Modern-Day Goddess Contemplations

1. Has there been a time in your life when you experienced some sort of trauma or misfortune, but now, when you look back, you realize it was a cosmic kick in the pants in the right direction?
2. Is something happening in your life right now that may actually be an opportunity for you to change?
3. Have you ever ignored your intuition and paid the consequences later?
4. Do you have at least one friend or person who would be there for you if you had an emergency?

What I Learned

Adversity can be an opportunity for a better life.
If something doesn't work out, it could be because there is a better path for you take.
Pay attention to cosmic clues.
Listen to your intuition.

A young goddess-in-training on vacation.

PART II:

The Modern-Day Goddess Basics

5

Meditation 101

Dear Diary:

The other day a girlfriend who hadn't talked to me in a few years called and commented how much calmer and more centered I sounded. She asked me what was my secret. I thought about her comment and decided it was my daily connection with my higher power and feminine self. While there are so many ways for a woman to do this, my modern-day goddess basics are meditation, laughter, yoga, positive self-talk, and Nordstrom's once-a-year sale.

I feel very grateful for meditation because it has quieted my mind, opened my heart and increased my self-love. Meditation has also helped me heal my body, mind and spirit. I've been meditating now for four years *and have found the serenity I experience in meditation stays with me throughout my day.*

But when I first started to explore meditation, it was a hair-raising experience.

As I entered the meditation classroom, I was greeted by Sky, our beautiful and centered instructor. She had long blonde hair, a warm smile and a gentle voice. "Welcome," she said gently, and continued infusing the air with a chakra-cleansing incense that reminded me of a garden filled with English lavender. Within minutes, the tranquil room was filled with other meditators in search of inner peace.

This was my first meditation experience. I had decided to explore meditation as a way to release stress, focus my mind and get in touch with my inner spirit—and to forget about my inner thighs, which I was trying to prevent from dimpling like the folds in Sky's robe.

Sky explained the proper sitting position (think pretzel) and lit a candle for us to focus on (think baked pretzel). She played some heavenly instrumental music that made me feel as if I was an angel floating on a cloud (think pretzel-lite). Next I concentrated on the breathing methods to clear my mind. It was the first time in months that I completely relaxed. The last time I felt that calm was when I drank too many cups of chamomile herb tea and fell into a deep sleep during an Enya concert.

The meditation progressed, and I began to feel sleepy. As

my chin drooped, I dozed off, drooling on my leotard. That's when my enlightened friend, SunRay, whispered in my ear, "You're snoring." This jerked me awake. "What? You think I'm boring?" I said loudly, forgetting where I was. Sun just looked at me and shook her head with a peaceful smile. The noise caused several meditators to briefly open their eyes. Next, Sky, who we later discovered was known outside of class as Ethel Johnson, came over to help. She suggested I repeat a mantra to prevent meditating myself into a coma. In meditation, one is supposed to fall awake and not asleep. Sky said that while a mantra helps some people stop their mind from racing, in this case it would help my mind stay alert. She explained the universal mantra is *Om,* which I immediately put to use. The snoring did stop, but I again fell into a very deep sleep. I remembered waking up after I toppled over with my knees in a gridlocked position onto the flickering candle we were supposed to focus on. There is nothing like the smell of singed hair mixed with lavender to snap you back to consciousness.

On my third try, I was determined to obtain some inner peace and inner joy. So I focused my mind back on the music and I made up a mantra that would definitely keep me awake. "*Om* George Clooney, *Om* Robert Redford, *Om* Mel Gibson." This chant put a big smile on my face. It really worked. In fact, I was one chant away from reenacting the famous Meg Ryan "Oh yes" scene in the movie *When Harry Met Sally* when the session came to a halt. Regardless, I still felt *very* satisfied and centered.

The serene feelings of my meditation stayed with me throughout the next day. Whenever something stressful occurred, like having to circle the block for ten minutes to find a parking space, I simply repeated the mantra *Ommmmmmm* to calm down. This gave me a sweet, peaceful feeling from connecting with my inner-self.

As I began to meditate for twenty minutes each day, I felt a strong centering in the midst of my busy day. Something was definitely happening, because when I saw one of my girl-friends, she asked me if I was in love. "Why do you say that?" I asked. "Because your eyes are sparkling and you look so relaxed." Then I answered in a calm, spiritual tone. "I am in love with . . . meditating. *Om* George Clooney, *Om* Robert Redford, *Om* Mel Gibson."

You May Need to Meditate to Relax If:

Your only moment of peace is when your cell phone battery goes dead.

You feel like your life is on the spin cycle.

Your brain feels like an overloaded computer disk that is "full."

Your "things to do" list looks like a volume from <u>War and Peace.</u>

You multi-task your multi-tasks.

You ar so stressed, the last time your inner child came out to play you left her with a baby-sitter.

The only mantra you've been repeating as you rush from appointment to appointment is: "Oh no, I'm late again."

You are running so far behind you have to listen to a relaxation tape while doing housework and errands.

You are so wound up that when you see a hummingbird hum, you want it to hurry.

The last time you sat through an entire meal was on the airplane—and that was because the seat belt sign was on.

The last time you met your inner-self was under sedation during a root canal.

You think your inner-self might resemble the Roadrunner instead of a goddess.

How to Meditate: Instructions

Over time, meditation can contribute to everything in your life, from inner peace and creativity to lower blood pressure. There are many books and tapes on meditation available at your local bookstore and library. But here are a few suggestions on how to get started. (See Goddess Books and Resources List in the back of the book for meditation books and tape suggestions.)

First, find a special time when you can be alone, and a special place such as a room or corner of a room. Some people like to get up a little earlier to make time for meditation. Some like to meditate at dawn and dusk to let any stress go, or even twice a day, at the beginning and end. Others like to meditate anytime, anywhere. You are free to choose. Try to get into a routine by meditating regularly in the same place once a day, even if it is only for ten minutes. This will help the mind know it is time to meditate. An ideal amount of time to stay in meditation is at least fifteen to twenty minutes a day. The more time you can spend meditating, the better.

Before you begin, make sure your body is comfortable. You can sit in a chair with your feet on the ground or on the floor with a pillow underneath you in a crossed-legged position. The most important thing is that you are comfortable and you keep your back straight.

Next, close your eyes and focus on your breath. As you breathe in and out, you can repeat a word like *peace, love* or a mantra such as *Om*, or *Om Namah Shivaya*—I honor my inner-self. The repetition will help quiet the mind.

When thoughts come up, just let them go. You can also bring yourself back to your center by repeating the mantra or sacred word. This is your time to relax. One way to release thoughts while meditating is to picture a small boat floating down a river, and every time a thought comes up, you place it into the boat to take it away.

Another method is to see yourself in a relaxing environment you enjoy, such as a beach where you let the sounds of the waves and the warmth of the sun relax you.

Yet another method is to listen to relaxing music and let yourself go. Classical music such as *Pachelbel's Canon in D* or any instrumental New Age music. (See Goddess Resource List for music suggestions.) Deepak Chopra, M.D., in the *Magical Mind, Magical Body* audiotape series, says when we are enjoying a piece of music, certain chemical changes in the body can be influenced—everything from lowering our heart rate to boosting our immune system to regulating the levels of hormones associated with stress. Whatever you choose, this is a time for you to unwind and nourish your inner-self. At the end of your meditation, you might want to visualize a successful day, give appreciation for the blessings in your life, ask for guidance and say an affirmation.

If you do begin meditating and stick with it, you will feel more serene, look more relaxed and build a strong relationship with your inner-self.

Inner-Wisdom Realization

You can experience an inner peace, self-love and an outer glow by awakening yourself through meditation.

Modern Day-Goddess Contemplations

1. Are you satisfied with the amount of quiet time you give yourself each day?
2. Do you rush from place to place and never give yourself a moment of peace?
3. How would an extra fifteen minutes of solitude affect your day?
4. What difference would a more peaceful mind and stronger inner-self make in your life?

5. When will you fit in some meditation time? Morning, noon or night?

6. What are some ways you could explore meditation this week? Can you buy a meditation tape, book or video, attend a meditation center or an adult education class?

What I Learned

Get a good night's sleep before taking a meditation course.

Keep candles at a safe distance.

If your mantra isn't working, chant something that brings you joy.

Meditation can also make you feel more lighthearted and look beautiful.

Daily meditation is an inner "spa" for your body, mind and soul.

Meditation is an effective way to connect with your higher power.

"Before Meditation"   *"During Meditation"*   *"After Meditation"*

Graphic design by Lynda Rae. Photo by Sally Franz.

6

Modern-Day Goddess Laughter

Dear Diary:

One of my favorite things in the whole universe to experience as a modern-day goddess is laughter. I know it's good for me because Norman Cousins boosted his immune system to fight an illness by watching funny movies and wrote about his success in his book, Anatomy of an Illness. So whenever I'm feeling stressed, I figure out a way to laugh and my world feels lighter.

To me, it's been a successful day if I have laughed or made someone else laugh. I've discovered that lightening up with humor can shift even the most serious day. For a modern-day goddess, lightheartedness is a valuable and sacred trait to be cherished in yourself and others.

I remember when a girlfriend of mine asked me if I had

always been funny. I didn't have an answer for her at first, so I asked myself. *When was the first time I started to feel "funny"? Besides the time I ate some bad sushi!*

I realized that as a child, I discovered humor was a great survival skill to diffuse stressful situations. But I think my funnybone became stronger when I was in my twenties and working as a reporter for a small, understaffed newspaper in Westport, Connecticut, a town where it has been rumored that F. Scott Fitzgerald once summered to write *The Great Gatsby*. And today, the rich and famous like Paul Newman and Martha Stewart call it home. I often wondered if Martha goes to Paul's house to borrow salad dressing when she runs out.

During my newspaper job, I worked under constant pressure for low pay. My paycheck at the end of each week was only $290—an amount that wouldn't even cover the cost of one Mercedes tire in Westport.

Real estate was at a premium, so I shared the rent on a house with three other women. At the newspaper, I shared a small room of computer terminals with three other reporters.

Our job was to cover the town's local news and its eccentric characters. We often cracked jokes about our lives and careers to ease the tension of writing six stories a week. It was the only way to survive the ongoing deadlines.

Our editor, a former tennis player in her fifties, was a colorful old-time resident who traveled everywhere with her loving canine, including a cross-country car trip with him in the front seat. The dog got pampered while we worked like dogs. As reporters, we joked that in our next life we wanted to come back as her dog.

On deadline day, we would rapidly pound the keyboards to get our stories out in time. In the midst of it all, our editor would walk into the middle of the newsroom, raise a pointed finger over her head and yell: "Five minutes to deadline." It always felt like a gunshot at the start of a fifty-yard dash.

My illustrious newspaper career consisted of covering the weekly town council meetings, which often ran until midnight or later, and one of the most coveted beats: garbage recycling. This was where my sense of humor helped get me through the week.

Recycling was big news, since it was just being introduced to the town of Westport. Before long, I was the Rona Barrett of trash. I wrote about paper versus plastic, 101 uses for six-pack plastic rings and the view from the various landfills. I even met the garbage police of the recycling center, who would take me aside and divulge in horror which wealthy residents hadn't properly recycled their soda cans.

I thought my big break had occurred when the editor said she was going to include a photo of me with one of my recycling stories. I did end up in print, but it was a photo of my butt. The photographer had captured me from "behind," when I bent over to hand a recycling bin to a local resident from the back of a waste management truck. While it bothered me at the time, I made it through that day and others by laughing about life's little jokes. Looking back, it was for the best that my first public photo was not a frontal view of me standing knee-deep in Styrofoam and old tuna cans.

As a reporter, I also wrote the obituaries—the cosmic recycling of death—"ashes to ashes, dust to dust." The obits rotated amongst the reporters, and it was our job to call around town to "dig up the facts." The only time I ever received a complaint was when I wrote about the town curmudgeon and a local resident phoned the paper to complain I made the "dead guy's obit too nice." It was a true Mary Tyler Moore moment.

All of this was not exactly what I had in mind when I was in journalism school studying until 2:00 A.M. But I survived, with hard work, little sleep and a good sense of humor. I also learned how to make deadlines and beg for extra editorial space. Eventually, some of my entertainment news stories and humor columns were printed when I wrote at night on my own time.

I stayed at the newspaper for as long as I could to get enough experience and not go into debt. The stress was starting to take its toll on my stomach. I wasn't the only one affected by the constant pressure. I knew it was time to leave when, in the middle of a deadline day, our editor suffered from an anxiety attack and was carried out on a stretcher. To this day, I still remember the paramedics whisking her past our desks in the newsroom and our ever-loyal editor lifting her head, pointing her finger into the air and saying: "Five minutes to deadline." It was then I learned the value of a good one-liner and exit.

My taste of comedy camaraderie in the newsroom gave me the courage to go out into the showbiz world. Several times a week, I moonlighted in comedy by traveling from Connecticut to New York to take classes in comedy writing and performing. I went to stand-up school, where the first thing they said was to "sit down and write something funny." There were exercises in how to write and speak with attitude about something that made you happy, frustrated or mad. The classic example was: "Don't you hate it when you lose one sock in the dryer? Where does it go? "

I soon discovered that with courage, good material and sensible shoes I could perform at comedy clubs in New York like Caroline's and Stand-Up New York. I also waitressed at a comedy club in Connecticut where the manager let me perform as long as none of my customers needed any drinks. Each weekend, I would rush up to the mike still wearing my waitress uniform of an apron, black skirt, white shirt, and black bow tie to tell jokes. I would start my act with: "Some of you might recognize me as your waitress, and as long as you don't order any drinks until I get off the stage, the management will let me perform for a few minutes. So please don't eat any peanuts!" The audiences thought it was a fun gimmick, and usually doubled my tips. It was then I learned truth is comedy.

I found that humor was also a great way to bond with people and heal relationships. It even became a form of laugh therapy between my Italian mother and me. When the world laughed with me about how she had been trying to marry me off since I was born, we both lightened up about the situation. At one point I would begin my act with "I'm almost thirty and single, which means my Italian family has officially declared me dead!" The pressure to get married used to bother me back then, but now my mother and I just laugh about it.

I remember my first paid comedy gig, for which I earned fifty dollars. That night, as I watched the comic before me, I got more and more nervous. His act consisted of sentences filled with expletives and lots of details about his latest sexual escapades. I felt like Audrey Hepburn preparing to follow

Andrew Dice Clay. For my opening act, I began with a teddy bear called Ted who I introduced as the perfect boyfriend because he was "cute, cuddly and a great listener." After my first laugh with Ted, I was able to relax. And the manager liked my "clean material" enough to book me for another show. It was a high being paid to make people laugh, but a low when all the bills came in and the money didn't go far.

Pursuing stand-up, waitressing, taking the train from New York to Connecticut at one in the morning, was a hard way to make a living. When I realized it would be a long journey to make the big bucks as a stand-up comedienne, I decided to use my humor to create and host my own local cable entertainment show with comedy segments and celebrity interviews. After a while, I asked for a sign from the universe if I should continue pursuing a career in the entertainment field, and the next week my show won a "most innovative cable award."

However, you don't have to win awards, write comedy or perform stand-up to add more humor into your life. There are so many outlets today to get a hit of humor: books, comic strips, movies, TV and funny friends. Be creative. I've brought laughter into my home by giving comedy potluck parties, where each guest brings a clip from his or her favorite comedian (no rubber chicken salad, please), and I co-founded a humor writer's group in Santa Barbara.

Laughing creates joy. And by surrounding yourself with humor you will feel more lighthearted.

When I brainstormed other ways to add humor into your life here's what I added to my list. You can visualize a Mount Rushmore of funny people like Lucille Ball, Robin Williams, Carol Burnett, Whoopi Goldberg and Bette Midler. Then, ask this panel of wit what they might say about a certain situation. Call up friends on the phone and exchange jokes. Get on an e-mail humor list. Watch ten minutes of the opening monologue of shows like Jay Leno, David Letterman, Rosie O'Donnell and Conan O'Brien. Take a comedy performing, writing or improvisation class. And why not create some laughing art, a poster board or a picture frame filled with funny cartoon strips and images of smiling people to remind yourself to laugh each day?

In the end, I've learned you can add more humor in your life through self-effort. And when things get really stressful, ask yourself what could be funny about your life if it was written as a sitcom or if you were watching someone else with your problems.

Inner-Wisdom Realization

God wants you to laugh and enjoy life. It's healthy and healing to lighten up with laughter. Lightheartedness is a sacred trait to be cultivated.

Modern-Day Goddess Contemplations

1. How can you get more in touch with your inner comic?
2. When was the last time you really laughed, and how did it make you feel?
3. What movies, books, friends and comedians make you laugh?

4. If you are upset about something, ask yourself the following questions:
    a. What will be funny about this situation when I look back on it?
    b. How can I lighten up about it now and save myself time?
    c. How would my lightheartedness improve the situation?
5. Who can I give the gift of laughter to today?

What I Learned

Guffawing is good.

I have an inner comic.

Look for ways to laugh at least once a day.

Humor is healing.

Humor is good for the soul.

Friends with great senses of humor are to be cherished.

If you want a good chuckle, have your sweetheart address you as "the great goddess." Or call your answering machine and tell yourself what a wonderful and witty goddess you are.

Humor can go too far, so here are times not to laugh:

Having a tooth drilled in the dentist's chair.
At a funeral.
At a silent meditation retreat.
In the library.
At a wedding ceremony.
When a police officer is writing you a speeding ticket.

A vital modern-day goddess moment of lightheartedness and laughter.

Photo by Annette Guionnet.

7

Goddess Self-Talk

Dear Diary:

Today I learned another millennium method to reach nirvana . . . it's through the power of affirmations. While talking to oneself has landed some people in a mental ward, it is now becoming acceptable, encouraged and even productive for a modern-day goddess. The difference is in what you say to yourself. For example, muttering obscenities is not attractive or recommended.

To learn about self-affirmations, I read a book by Shad Helmstetter, Ph.D., called *What to Say When You Talk to Yourself*. Shad says you can decrease stress, feel more peaceful and manifest your life's desire through your thoughts. He also suggests you record a tape to play each day with positive self-talk. The phrases should be said in the present tense as if everything you desire has already occurred.

It sounded simple, so I decided to experiment. One day, I gathered all of my positive-thinking books and had an affirmation festival. Instead of sayings like: "I'm having a very bad hair day. I hate PMS. I feel bloated and life sucks," I created: "I am a modern-day goddess in touch with my feminine power, strength and courage. I am divinely guided and protected. I now have a healthy, fit body. I'm blessed beyond my wildest dreams, and I'm grateful to Midol!"

I looked through the books for more sayings that appealed to me, like: "I'm feeling more beautiful every day, and I love and appreciate myself unconditionally" from Louise Hay's *Empowering Women* book. And one of my favorites: "I now expect unexpected income," from *Prosperity Aerobics* by Cary Bayer. For this one, I prepared myself and put my sneakers by the bed in the event I needed to sprint to the bank with a large cash deposit.

One of my self-talk practicing friends told me his theory on how all of this works. Supposedly, by constantly repeating what has not yet happened, your mind will fill this void by attracting your heart's desire.

The mind is a powerful tool! So I added a self-talk session to my daily fifteen-minute goddess routine—meditation, prayer, a quick visualization of a successful day and requests for divine intervention. Next, I recorded these on a cassette for repeat playing while driving around beautiful Santa Barbara. Then I hopped into my car to do errands. First stop—Pierre La Fond's, a popular cafe that attracts a cross-culture of Santa Barbara citizens and Los Angeles visitors on the weekends.

There I ran into comedic genius Jonathan Winters, who always makes me laugh and usually has a crowd standing around him while he ad libs hilarious comedy. I had interviewed Jonathan before for a radio show, so when he asked me how I was, I couldn't resist telling him about my self-talk experiment. His response: "I tried that positive stuff once, but I started talking back to myself. I'd say: 'You're wonderful. No you're not, get in the car.'"

We both laughed. Jonathan then did an impression of my mother with an Italian accent. He was so funny, I accidentally spit out my no-sugar, no-fat, no-caffeine, why-bother, frozen mochachino. I was quite embarrassed and apologized. I found myself thinking *I am feeling more stupid every second* but quickly changed it to *I am feeling more beautiful each day*. This allowed me to see the humor in the situation and remark that I could now audition for David Letterman's stupid human tricks. Jonathan loved it and we both had a good laugh before he drove away.

After I cleaned myself up, I spotted SunRay, one of my highly evolved environmentalist friends. SunRay, formerly Gertrude Shapiro and soon to be SunRay Montgomery, was given her name by a spiritual master—a name she readily accepted as replacement for Gertrude. SunRay took me over to see her beautiful new white Mercedes convertible. I couldn't believe it. The last time I saw her, she was driving an old Volkswagen with a bumper sticker that said, "Visualize World Peace." Obviously she had also been visualizing some automotive peace.

As she ordered a chai tea, SunRay told me when her boyfriend proposed with a ring, he also gave her the car as an engagement present. "It can happen to you," she said as she sleeked into her car and out of the parking space. "Just visualize it, believe it and chant it daily. Remember the Janis Joplin lyrics, 'Oh Lord, Won't You Buy Me a Mercedes-Benz.' Well, it works." I watched as SunRay zoomed off with a big smile and the wind blowing in her hair.

I felt a bit down as I walked back to my dented 1989 Ford Mustang clunker with 150,000 miles and a convertible top stuck in a semi-upright position. To cheer myself up, I drove straight to the automotive store and bought a Mercedes-Benz hood ornament, which I duct-taped to the hood. I then chanted nonstop: "I now have a beautiful Mercedes." For a final touch, I applied a bumper sticker that said, "My other car is a Mercedes."

As I drove around town in my goddess transporter, I continued to play my affirmation tape. At a red light, I turned up the volume and repeated in a smoldering voice: "I am a beautiful, cherished, outrageous and sexy goddess." I was really getting into it when I felt someone watching me. In the car next to me, I saw an older man in a Porsche with slicked-back hair, gold-capped teeth and a slippery smile, grinning at me as I finished my affirmation with gusto: "I am a beautiful, cherished, outrageous and sexy goddess." Without missing a beat, he said leering at me: "Take me baby, I'm yours!" Shocked, I blurted out, "I can't talk to you. My boyfriend, who has a black belt in karate, is waiting for me at the next corner. And I'm late!" He hit the gas and left skid marks. I quickly added to my affirmations: "I am a goddess who attracts only wonderful, healthy and highly evolved men."

Several miles later at the next stoplight, I turned down the volume on my affirmations for fear of any more misdirected affirmations. I also worried that an innocent man could be at a crosswalk and get one of my goddess affirmations stuck in his head like a song. Then he would walk around all day repeating, "I'm turning into a more beautiful goddess each day." And I would feel responsible for messing up his testosterone level.

At the next light, I quietly repeated another affirmation to myself: "I am feeling more centered and beautiful every day. God is my lavish and constant supply of abundance." Abudance can be defined as success in all areas of your life such as health, wealth, love, career spirituality, relationships and perfect self-expression.

As I waited, I noticed a farmer from the nearby outdoor market crossing the street toward me. He stopped at my car and handed me a beautiful bouquet of peach-colored roses. "These are a gift for you," he said. "Because you are beautiful and you should be surrounded by beautiful things." I was stunned and offered to pay him. He refused, and I drove home blissfully happy—talking to myself all the way!

When I arrived back at my cozy goddess apartment, there was a message on my answering machine from a magazine editor who said a goddess article I wrote had been accepted and I was going to be paid four thousand dollars. Wow! The affirmation, "I expect unexpected income" was really working!

I immediately thought about tithing to keep my prosperity flowing.

I remembered that Edwene Gaines, an inspiring prosperity goddess and lecturer, said you should tithe 10 percent of your income to something that gives you spiritual food. Tithing contributes to providing a continuous flow of prosperity. I thought to myself: *Now, I know where I would tithe for my nourishing food—Kenny Rogers Roasters. A place where four hundred dollars would buy a lot of chickens. But for spiritual food, I'll give two hundred dollars to my meditation center and the other two hundred dollars to my Unity church.*

Inspired toward more abundance, I quickly made up two more affirmations. One for my career: "I am now a bestselling author whose books and TV show are inspiring millions of women!" And the other for my love life: "I now have a great mate who is spiritual, romantic, kind, honest, loyal, loves to cuddle and has a great sense of humor."

I repeated these while tidying up my sacred living space. Every hour or so, I would open the front door to check for any men or book contracts. There was nothing. Next I lit some incense and candles to invite additional goddess vibes into my home. Nothing again. I waited for a while by the door then sat down to write the last page of my goddess book proposal.

An hour later, my doorbell rang and I rushed to open it. It wasn't Mr. Right or Mr. Book Contract—instead, it was a Girl Scout selling cookies. Never wanting to say no to a future goddess entrepreneur, I bought five boxes of chocolate mint cookies. I quickly began sampling the cookies, which broke my no-sugar goddess diet rule. No matter, it was one of my lesser rules. The doorbell rang again. This time, I thought it might be the mailman. I opened the door, completely unaware of my chocolate-mint-crumb and soy-milk mustache. Luckily, I remembered to wipe it off when I saw what was on my doorstep. It was a tall, attractive male with an athletic build, blue-green eyes and a divine smile. He introduced himself as Michael, my new neighbor. Michael had just moved in and wanted to know where the recycling bins were—something I was able tell him, along with trash tips, because of my supreme knowledge of recycling. I pointed out the containers and promptly invited him in for cookies. We chatted. He seemed to be quite a conscious male, spiritual (thank goddess), healthy, happy and the owner of a small but successful book publishing company. I told him I was a writer working on this book, and he offered to look at my manuscript. I agreed to meet him for lunch later in the week, even though we discovered later we were astrologically incorrect; his Scorpio moon cusped my Leo sun.

After he left, I gave thanks to my inner-goddess and Shad Helmstetter, the self-talk author. I danced around the room to Enya, my favorite goddess music. I reflected. Five years of writing about my goddess-enlightenment adventures might actually pay off, my new neighbor turns out to be a publisher and I have a beautiful bouquet of fragrant roses on my table. I felt divine.

As I grow older, I am learning to accept myself unconditionally. Sure, it's wonderful manifesting my goals, but it's appreciating the journey that really matters. I decided to love my car unconditionally, too. I knew it got me around town to the best of its ability, and a new car would arrive in my future when the stars deemed it so. In that moment, I felt compassion for myself and my Mustang, and removed the Mercedes hood ornament.

Inner-Wisdom Realization

You have the power to self-talk your way to a better life.

Modern-Day Goddess Contemplations

1. Are you aware of what you say to yourself on a daily basis? Is it kind, loving and positive, or something you would never say to a person you loved—or to anyone else for that matter?
2. Write down a negative thought you have and turn it into a positive affirmation as if it has already happened. For example: "I am so stressed out, I can't get everything done" to "I am now organized, relaxed and efficient."
3. Practice your affirmation during the day by posting it on your mirror, in your car or writing it down and carrying it with you.
4. How would repeating this affirmation have an impact on your life?

What I Learned

Your thoughts create your reality.

Affirmations can create a beautiful goddess life.

Watch out for misdirected affirmations.

Be conscious about what you ask for because you just might get it.

8

Yogacize

Dear Diary:

Today I discovered the benefits of doing yoga. I was not only able to get in touch with my inner-self, but also my inner thighs.

I must admit the first time I took a yoga class I had a little performance anxiety. But it eventually went away as the postures helped me relax when I realized the other students in my beginning class might have the same thing, too, since most of us were yoga virgins.

f a modern-day goddess isn't careful, stress can creep into her life, zap her of energy and leave her feeling as burnt out as a campfire marshmallow. But there is a simple and inexpensive way to nurture a stressed-out soul when your budget doesn't include the fantasy of a massage therapist on call. It's called yoga, and it is a practice that nurtures the spirit, lets the body relax and quiets the mind.

Yoga is an act of self-love. While I may not always want to do it, afterwards I have a serene glow and a centered feeling that reminds me of the inner peace I feel after making love with my beloved. How's that for an irresistible spin on yoga? Now that I've gotten your attention, I encourage you to check out some form of this ancient practice.

In one article I read about taking care of the body as the temple for the soul, yoga was said to help with everything from strengthening muscles and flexibility to balancing your body, mind, spirit and possibly even astrological planets. It was also noted that over six million people now practice yoga—which is the same number of people who have obtained inner peace and a sense of serenity from purchasing the anti-theft club device for their car.

Before I actually took a yoga class, it seemed that everywhere I went someone mentioned yoga. And in goddess land, when you hear the same thing mentioned several times, it is considered a message from either God, the universe or your grandmother, who is transmitting a telepathic telegram to you from heaven.

But my most powerful "just do yoga" message was delivered from a higher power through the voice of my girlfriend Aura. It occurred when she and I were shopping at the Nordstrom's anniversary sale. We were in the midst of trying on piles of fabulous clothes marked between 50 to 75 percent off. Our dressing room had dresses, shirts and pants strewn everywhere. This was a major shop till you drop sale, and we didn't want to miss anything. I was ready to pass out with exhaustion from trying everything on, deciding what fit, what didn't and going back to the racks to look for more.

I was amazed that my girlfriend Aura had boundless energy and continued on like the Energizer bunny. I, on the other hand, flopped down on a pile of clothes and deeply sighed. "Aura," I said. "I'm feeling stressed and in need of a nap." Her response was: "Cindy love, I think you need to increase your stamina and release some stress. Have you tried yoga? It works for me."

While driving home, I thought about her comment and heard the word *Yoga! Yoga! Yoga!* chanting in my head. Obviously, my inner goddess was determined that I begin. So I stopped off at my local video store to find a yoga tape. It was the perfect way to explore yoga without embarrassing myself in public with the somewhat complex-looking poses. After all the testimonials I had heard, my hopes of alleviating my daily-living stress were high. But on my first attempt, I didn't relax at all. It seems that my leotard was too tight and I was distracted by the wedgie it gave me during certain poses. Then when I tried to sit in the full-lotus pretzel position, my knees once again locked up.

Of course, that was when the Fed Ex man rang my doorbell. I attempted to unlock my knees, but instead I dragged myself to the door. "Down here," I said when he asked me to sign for a box of aromatherapy oils I had ordered. I determined him to be a very polite Fed Ex man when he pretended it was just in another's day work to see a three-foot woman answering the door while sitting.

After he left, I traveled back to the living room on my knees and prayed to the goddess of yoga to unlock me. It took a few minutes, but it worked. It was then I realized my yoga practice should not be attempted without proper supervision. So I called my local athletic club. The girl at the end of the phone read off my choices: "We have power yoga, gentle yoga, beginning yoga, intermediate and advanced yoga, Kundalini yoga, Hatha yoga, yoga for couples, yoga for youths and—for the holistic pet owners—yoga for dogs!"

Since I was a beginner and didn't have a dog, I decided on the beginning yoga class. This time I made sure to wear loose clothing. When I entered the yoga room, the lights were dim and the rows of bodies passed out on mats looked like an adult nap session. I quietly placed a yoga mat on the floor and surveyed the room. Our class had an assortment of students, ranging from what looked like a female student wearing a sweatshirt with a UCSB (University of California–Santa Barbara) logo, to a stressed-out entrepreneur with a bejeweled cellphone by her mat side, to a hard body still wearing his weight-lifting belt around his waist, to a young mom wearing a T-shirt that said "I'm a natural birth mom . . . support midwives." There was also a serene and wise-looking silver-haired elder woman and, much to my surprise, several attractive men—an older, tanned executive who looked as if he just stepped off the golf course, a ponytailed creative type and a cuddly teddy bear lookalike. I thought to myself, *Even men are now braving the yoga frontier for balance, or to perhaps get in touch with their feminine side, their inner goddess, or to meet a goddess.*

Our instructor introduced herself as Joy and sat effortlessly in a full-pretzel lotus position. She also demonstrated how we could sit in a half-pretzel position, which I was grateful for because of the quick escape and anti-locking possibilities. Joy led us into a series of deep cleansing breaths. Even though it sounded like the breathing of a scuba diver being followed in a Jacques Cousteau film, I followed along and felt my body immediately beginning to calm down.

Throughout the class, I attempted to keep up with the various yoga poses. Many of them had names that related to a warrior, animal or baby.

For me, the downward dog position where you get down on all fours with your head on the floor in an inverted V was a bit strenuous. I thought this position wasn't for humans and should stay where it might have originated from, in the yoga-for-dogs class. What did they have the dogs doing? The upward human position, where they have to stand up tall like us? In the midst of my musing, I struggled in the downward dog position and let my hair flop forward like a sixties music groupie. When I turned my head to the side, Mr. Ponytailed Creative Type winked at me. I chuckled, he waved. When our instructor said to think and act like a dog, my classmate got up on his hind legs, looked at me with doggy eyes, and bent his hands up like paws. I couldn't help but burst out laughing. At this point, everyone turned to look at us. I blushed and Mr. Ponytail playfully wiggled his backside and barked. A bit embarrassed at disrupting the class, I seized the moment and patted him on the head. It shifted the energy and everyone joined in laughing—including our teacher. To regain the serene atmosphere, she rang a large gong with a plush stick to restore some quiet.

Our class continued as we attempted to contort our bodies through various poses such as the cobra, where you arch back like a snake, or the warrior pose, where you stand as if you are a samurai lunging at a sword. My two favorite poses were the child's pose and the fetal position. My inner child was having a great time without being in a Lamaze or fetal fitness class. The reason I love these poses is because they are the only two positions in the entire class where you get to rest except for the ending meditation. For the child's pose you kneel with your arms stretched out, touching the floor as if you are bowing to a Buddha. Once I learned this pose, I substituted it if a position was too difficult and I needed a break. For the fetal position, you lay on your side with your arm and legs pulled into your body as if you were still in the womb.

I glanced around and thought how courageous and vulnerable everyone was to be willing to try the postures. I think we also bonded as a group because there is something vulnerable about a bunch of grown adults attempting poses that make them look like they are regressing back to childhood.

The more poses I completed, the more the muscles in my body begin to relax, any energy blocks became unlocked and my body began to tingle. I actually felt a tender loving feeling traveling throughout my body like the afterglow a goddess feels after an orgasm! (No, I'm not an oversexed goddess, but it's the only reference I can think of.) Everyone in the class looked as if their faces were softening; we all looked more attractive. Perhaps it is the magic powers of yoga endorphins, which create a loving feeling. After all, I am told that Tantra, a spiritual and conscious way of lovemaking, has its origins in a form of yoga.

For the end of our class, Joy told us to lie down, meditate

for a few minutes and give thanks to the yogis. What yogis did she mean? Did she mean my own personal wise inner yogi or the cartoon characters Yogi Bear and Boo-Boo?

I was too alpha zoning to be able to speak. So I thanked them all. When class was over I felt pure bliss. What a healing and satisfying release. As I stood up, I felt my mind, body and spirit shift into balance.

I enjoyed yoga so much I signed up for a month of classes. My inner calm must have been reflected on my face because I ran into a girlfriend at the club who said I was glowing and must be in love! Yes, I was! I was having a huge love affair, this time with myself and yoga. I was grateful, so I gave thanks to everyone like they do at the Oscars—Joy, my instructor; my inner yogi; Yogi Bear and Boo-Boo; my parents; and, of course, the Academy members.

Inner-Wisdom Realization

You can stay fit, flexible and balanced through yoga.

Modern-Day Contemplations

1. How would practicing yoga even once a week contribute to your overall well-being?
2. How can you add yoga into your week? Perhaps through a class, a video, an early morning TV show, several poses from a book?

3. What would it mean to you to have a yoga glow?

What I Learned

Don't practice yoga without proper supervision.
Wear loose clothing.
Yoga can balance your body, mind and spirit.
Yoga can give you a wonderful, relaxed yoga glow.

Yogacizing in nature.

Photo by Jenna Haudesty.

9

Modern-Day Goddess Shopping

Dear Diary:

Today, I discovered Nirvana at Nordstrom! The ideal retail ashram for my lofty mission of finding the perfect pumps and attaining great bliss. While I do know there are ways to pamper myself for little or no money—from beach talk-walks with a girlfriend to a relaxing bath to painting my toenails fire-engine red—sometimes, a modern-day goddess just needs to embrace the concept that she deserves abundance by spending some cold cash on herself. So that's what I did. Today I hopped in the car and went shopping. Okay, it wasn't as impulsive as it sounds. For weeks, I had actually been visualizing a pair of golden power pumps I wanted for an important publishing meeting. They were a reward to get me through a crucial writing deadline. And I felt I really scored when I found them. So, here is a play-by-play account of my visit to Nordstrom.

y first step into Nordstrom deposited me directly into their exciting and sprawling shoe department. I felt mesmerized by their large selection of shoes adorned with bows, flowers, jungle stripes, thongs and platform shoes in colors like fuchsia, turquoise and ginger. At first, my heart jumped for joy as I fell in love with over a dozen or more pairs of shoes on display. But when I realized I only had the money for one pair, I had to sit down on the fitting couch to calm myself. Of course, I had my charge card in my purse, but I believe a modern-day goddess should try to stick to her spending plan, so she can enjoy her abundance without the guilt of debt. Not wanting to feel deprived, I made a note to myself to get a Nordstrom catalog and put photos of the shoes on my F.U.N. (Fabulous Unlimited Nirvana) Board, which is a posterboard I fill with all wonderful things I would like to manifest in my life. It is a technique that has worked successfully for me in the past. (See instructions at the end of the chapter on how you can create your own F.U.N. board.)

On the couch I took a few deep-centering breaths to access my inner shopping goddess and practice mindfulness—the art of quieting the mind and focusing on the present moment to bring myself back into the shoe department and my body. Next, I repeated my shopping mantra, "Ommmm dear shopping goddess—please help me find the perfect gold pumps that make me feel like an elegant modern-day goddess. Ommm dear goddess, please help me find them in my size, so they don't give me blisters. Omm dear goddess, please let them be on sale."

When I was done, I stood up from the couch, confidently walked toward the on-sale shoe racks and mumbled my mantras to myself. Surrounded by a variety of left shoes, I stood very still until I heard one calling me. I rapidly searched the display racks and spotted a golden pump that seemed to glow with a great aura. It was sparkling like Dorothy's red ruby slippers. My divine shoe was the sleekest, most sophisticated gold pump in a size eight, at 50 percent off. I almost shrieked out loud with joy. But the pressure was still on because it had to fit.

I quickly hurried back to the couch as I prayed to my inner-goddess shopper. Then I took a deep breath and slipped on the shoe. When it fit I felt like Cinderella. Best of all the power pumps made my left leg look like it belonged to a supermodel. A leg good enough to be photographed stepping out of a limousine onto a red carpet for a movie premiere. Okay, this all might be a bit of a stretch since I'm only five-four. But I did feel very glamorous.

With the pump on my left foot, I looked again in a full-length mirror, and started to think about what my life would be like with a matching pair of golden shoes. It wasn't easy to do at first, with my right foot lifted like a flamingo, but soon my imagination soared. First I was Aphrodite, the beautiful Greek goddess of love, dressed in a flowing off-white silk and lace gown with my golden pumps peeking out from under-neath. Then, I was in a conference room dressed in a stylish cream-colored business suit, a gold silk shirt and my match-ing gold pumps. As I successfully presented my ideas, the people at the meeting were smiling and nodding in approval. Next, I was Audrey Hepburn in *Breakfast at Tiffany's* sashaying my way through an elegant black-tie affair wearing a little black dress with gold trim and of course my golden goddess pumps. My perfect pumps gave me a real lift as I imagined myself laughing, dancing and having wonderful conversations with intriguing people—especially men.

Finding the exact shoes I wanted, on sale, that actually fit, made me feel as if I had won something. I was so happy I did a victory tour lap around the shoe rack holding my pump in the air like the Statue of Liberty. When I made it to the check-out counter, I plunked the pump down—ready to claim my victory and the matching right shoe. After I paid for my purchase, I triumphantly exited the store through the sliding glass doors, lifted my Nordstrom bag to the heavens and said "YES!" It felt as if my inner shopping goddess and I had really scored. But most of all it was a personal victory because I took action and claimed some of the abundance each person deserves as their birthright.

Inner-Goddess Realization

Our creator wants us to prosper. Treating yourself to something special can make you feel worthy of abundance, which can then open the door to attract even more abundance. You deserve to have abundance and happiness in all areas of your life—health, wealth, love, relationships, peace of mind, self-expression and even the perfect footwear! Repeat this affirmation daily and watch for results: The universal spirit of abundance provides lavishly for me now!

Modern-Day Goddess Contemplations

1. When was the last time you treated yourself to some great shoes or a piece of clothing?
2. What is something that makes you feel abundant?
3. Can you remember a time when you focused on something that nurtured you and you were able to manifest it with ease?
4. Do you feel you deserve abundance and prosperity?
5. How do you use your intuition throughout the day?

What I Learned

Just like Dorothy in the *Wizard of Oz*, I always had the power to create what I wanted, by believing, clicking my heels three times and saying: "There is no place like Nordstrom."

The power of focusing with a clear and quiet mind.

The power of the perfect pump.

How to be an intuitive shopper.

That you can experience nirvana in an everyday situation.

The power of abundant living includes all areas of your life.

How to Create a F.U.N. (Fabulous Unlimited Nirvana) Board

Okay, Goddesses, it's time to experience some F.U.N. (Fabulous Unlimited Nirvana) by dreaming big, cutting out images of what you want in your life and pasting them onto a board.

I can tell you it really does work. With the help of my F.U.N. Board, I've manifested lots of wonderful things in my life that have nurtured me, from travel and money to a publishing contract and romance. (See chapter 12 Goddess Self-Love—Dating Yourself, to read about how I put creative visualization into action for a great date.)

Before I begin, I like to write down what I want to manifest. Successful prosperity author Catherine Ponder says in her book, *The Prosperity Secret of the Ages*, that declaring your intention is an important step. She explains that "Your written words go out into the ethers of the universe to work through people, circumstances, and events, to open the way for your deserved good."

There are different names for what I call a F.U.N. Board. Catherine Ponder calls it a Wheel of Fortune. Cary Baker, author of *Prosperity Aerobics*, calls it a Treasure Map. Baker says, "The purpose behind the Treasure Map creation and daily gazing is to plant images of success into your creative and fertile unconscious." He also suggests adding this line at the bottom of your visualization board: "This or something better now manifests for me in safe and totally harmonious ways for all concerned." While the names for the board may change, its purpose remains the same.

Remember to think carefully about what you put on your board because you will probably get it, so have fun with it. Do you want to travel to Hawaii, write a book, become a gourmet cook, a published author, go to a spa, relax more, become a mother, an entrepreneur, get your dream car, dream mate, dream house, dream wardrobe, get in shape? Just put it all on your F.U.N. Board, take action toward your goal and see what happens.

To create your own F.U.N. Board you'll need scissors, a glue stick, a posterboard, magazines, travel brochures, mail-order catalogs and a happy photo you like of yourself. Once you've collected your working materials, put on some soothing music and have a cutting festival. If you don't know where to start, think of images that correspond to the different areas in your life: spiritual, career/creative work, financial, love, family, social life, romance, health, beauty, fitness, transportation, etc. or just select images you are drawn to. It's also important to include a happy photo of you on an image of something you know you would really enjoy.

My F.U.N. Board also includes color copies of money so I will have a nest egg and the finances to maintain what I manifest, photos of people I admire, and images of women relaxing so I will manifest enough time to nurture myself and enjoy the process. In the center of the board, I also include a photo of something that represents the divine source of the universe and the higher consciousness of my spirit that will assist me in creating my abundance. (For example, a photo of a spiritual master, angels, goddesses, your all-loving dog!)

Once you're finished, celebrate a job well done by looking over your F.U.N. Board and feeling the emotions of what your life will be like if you manifest your desires. Then surrender to the idea that the universe will have it show up in the best possible way for you. Gaze at the images on your board or think of them in your mind daily. Your dreams and wishes are sacred, so only share your F.U.N. Board with those you feel will be supportive of your visions. You can also have a F.U.N.

night with your friends and create your vision boards together for one or all areas of your life. A great time for this is after the New Year, before a birthday, or any time you need a boost or clarity in your life. Try it and write or e-mail me at the address at the back of the book with your successes. And remember to have F.U.N.

A F.U.N. (Fabulous Unlimited Nirvana) Board.

10

Glorious Goddess Girlfriends

Dear Diary:

Lately, I've been thinking about how important glorious goddess girlfriends are to a modern-day goddess' life and sanity. To me, the ideal girlfriend is someone who is kind, trustworthy, accepting and nurturing with a good sense of humor. Someone with whom I feel lucky to share the sacred bond of female friendship. Friendship can also be love and compassion in action—which is exactly what I experienced today.

"Did you bring the aromatherapy stuff?" asked Isabella, who is a very expressive nine-year-old and daughter of my girlfriend Charlotte. "I sure did," I answered. It was 7 A.M., I was a bit sleepy, but still standing upright as I walked into the hospital waiting room with a bag filled with pillows, an aromatherapy diffuser, oils and angel cards. "Where's your mom?" I asked. "She's in the cafe getting some tea and said to tell you she'll be back in a few minutes."

I sat down and waited for Charlotte to return. The waiting room had a clinical ambience which was intensified by the cement white walls and fluorescent light. Across the room, sitting in uncomfortable-looking chairs, were several sad-looking people waiting anxiously for their loved ones in surgery.

I closed my eyes for a few moments and thought about how women can be a great source of comfort to each other in time of need—something I experienced from several female friends when I was recovering from surgery for a broken wrist. Last week, when Charlotte had learned her husband Paul would be having surgery to discover if a lump was cancerous or benign, she immediately called her girlfriends for support. The message on my answering machine said: "I know I'll be anxious when he is in surgery for three hours, so I want to have a cocoon of friends with me in the waiting room. I would love to have you there and any laughter or aromatherapy oils you can provide would be appreciated. Thanks."

That moment, Charlotte entered the room. As an expressive arts therapist she often dressed in expressive clothes. Today she was wearing a colorful shirt and her signature orange chiffon scarf around her neck. "Helloooooo, I'm so glad you're here," said Charlotte in a musical French-German accent. "It means so much to me." We hugged as she introduced me to her other two girlfriends, Vanessa, a graphic artist and Sabina, an acupuncturist.

I gave Charlotte my aromatherapy diffuser and she asked the waiting-room attendant if she could plug it in by her desk. The older woman seemed surprised at first, but then quickly said yes. As I watched the interaction, I didn't think she would say no; after all this was California—home of alternative healing. And once the attendant got a whiff of the calming scents, she was thrilled, especially when she discovered they cleared up her sinuses.

Sabina, Vanessa and I sat down around Charlotte. Her daughter, Isabella was contently playing a board game nearby. It was a comforting sight to see the small community we had created in the waiting room. Together, we chatted and caught up on what was happening in our lives. We patiently waited for the time to pass and the moment when Paul's surgeon would come into the waiting room to let us know if the surgery was a success.

We all looked up each time we saw a surgeon dressed in green scrubs enter the waiting room to talk to the appropriate loved ones. At one point there were so many doctors coming and going, I felt like an expectant family member waiting in a maternity ward to hear about the birth of triplets. So I turned to Charlotte and asked: "What will we do if your husband's doctor comes in and tells us 'It's a boy!'?" We all howled with laughter and the anxiousness of the moment was released.

As we continued to wait for the news of the surgery, we decided to take a moment to pray by giving thanks, asking for protection and speaking of the surgery as a success. I was asked to say the prayer: "We now give thanks that Paul's doctors be guided throughout the procedure, that he is protected by white light, that the surgery is a success, that the lump they remove is not cancerous and that Paul heals quickly so he can thoroughly enjoy his family." "And the chocolate chip cookies we made!" added Isabella.

The people on the other side of the waiting room were looking as if they wanted to join our group for a boost. My heart went out to them and I felt a yearning to include them into our goddess circle of love and friendship. In that moment, a woman from an entrepreneurial group I once belonged to got up and came over to visit. She seemed drawn to our energy and told us her husband was having surgery for a bone injury. We shared our smiles and love knowing how hard it is to face these times alone.

It was then I thought about how important it is for people not to feel alone during a life challenge. And I remembered being told that in certain cultures, the entire family goes to the doctor's office when someone is ill to lend support.

I brought myself back to our friendship circle and asked Charlotte about the teddy bear that was nearby. "It's for Paul from Isabella," she said. Isabella picked up the bear and hugged it. "It has lots of good energy because I slept with it for two nights to get it ready for him," Isabella said.

Charlotte recounted the whole experience of the doctors, the news, and the way Paul thoroughly researched everything. His efforts paid off when he located a wonderful anesthesiologist who used hypnosis to command the body to properly heal. The family also spent the morning together before Paul went into surgery. At 5 A.M. in the hospital room, instead of watching television like the nurse suggested while his valium took effect, he spent the time with his family.

Dressed in a terrycloth robe, Paul put on his favorite Chopin music and invited his wife and daughter with bear in tow—to dance along with him. It was a touching moment for all.

To pass the time in the waiting room, we discussed what friendship meant in our lives. Vanessa said life has all kinds of challenges and friendship helps you cope. Charlotte said that her friends are lifelines of support. "They are what keep me going and not feeling alone."

I said my friends provided me with a solid foundation that keeps me grounded, loved and lighthearted. And good friends give you a chance to reveal your true inner-self without worry.

Sabina said: "You can ask friends for help when needed without feeling guilty or embarrassed." I flashed back to when my wrist had been in a cast for weeks, and one of my girlfriends graciously agreed to pluck my unruly eyebrows. That was definitely true friendship.

In the book *Girlfriends*, Carmen Renee Berry and Tamara Traeder, say "There's nothing that warms the heart more than knowing you have a loyal friend, someone who will stand by you no matter what." I think a good friend can give a woman the support and acceptance she may not have received in childhood. And, I feel friends can also be a second family of souls who come into our lives to guide and teach us. While some friends are meant to be with us for life, others may be here for only a short time to provide a lesson and then move on. Regardless, Doctor Dean Ornish, author of *Love and Survival*, says whether it's called love or support, it can make a significant difference in a person's life and their longevity.

In that moment, Paul's surgeon entered the waiting room,

not carrying a baby boy, but a big smile that said everything was okay. When he told us the surgery had been a success, we thanked him and hugged each other in a glorious goddess girlfriend cocoon feeling our goddess power might have made a difference. And the next day, Paul was told the lump was benign. Thank goddess!

Inner-Wisdom Realization

You can contribute a lot to others by sharing your heart, knowledge, stories, wisdom and wit in times of need and celebration. Fabulous friends are priceless treasures to be cherished.

Modern-Day Goddess Contemplations

1. How have you and your girlfriends contributed to each other?
2. What have you and your girlfriends shared?
3. What qualities do you think make a good friend? Do you feel you are a good friend?
4. Do you give yourself the treat of connecting with a girl-friend at least once a week?

5. Is there a girlfriend you've lost touch with who you can reconnect with by making a phone call or writing a letter?
6. Do you wish you had more nurturing girlfriends? Where might you meet some?

What I've Learned

Girlfriends are great and important to a goddess' well-being. Girlfriends are a goddess gift to be cultivated and appreciated. An adult play date with a girlfriend can boost your spirits for a week and give you something to look forward to.

The Gifts of Female Friendship

As an appreciation exercise, I wrote down some of the many things I've shared over the years with girlfriends. Here's my list. Take time to make a list of your friendship gifts.

Laughter, smiles, hugs, tears, words of encouragement, PMS woes, life visions, fears, brainstorming, meditation, yoga, smoothies, prayers, adult play dates, shopping trips, the gym, manicures, hot rollers, nurturing tips, compassionate listening, fears, joys, travel, books, chick flicks, jokes, convertibles, uplifting answering machine messages, a place to stay, writing, letters, cards, counseling phone calls, bad-date details, heartbreak stories, empowering talks, good-date details, great relationship details, talks about a day of rest at the beach, dreams of a day of rest at the beach, an actual day of rest at the beach, sunset beach walks, sandboxes, Barbie dolls, business savvy, conflict resolution tips, workshops, creative dreams, seeing the big picture, seeing the details, seeing the life lessons, great lunches, help with moving, help with healing, help with the ups and downs of life, help with coloring your hair, mom stories, family stories, love stories, relationship tips, truth telling, decorating tips, tablecloths, recipes, cooking, meals, Feng Shui advice, aromatherapy scents, gifts, flowers, gardening tips, lots of advice, FUN!

PART III:

Modern-Day Goddess Love

11

Mi Amore,
Mama Mia

Dear Diary:

While most of my life my Italian mother has been pushing me toward the altar, I've been meditating and creating my own meditation altar.

Today I was on the phone with my mother, and when I told her about my recent success at a business meeting, she said: "That's nice. But was the man you had the meeting with single?" I felt frustrated, so I chanted <u>Om, om, om my God</u> to myself until I started laughing.

Our conversation reminded me of a remark a therapist once said to give me a compassionate view of my mother-daughter marital-status situation. He said certain mothers don't feel they've succeeded in raising their children until they are married off. And each woman needs to decide what's right for her. It was then I learned a modern-day goddess has a choice to get hitched and *needs to decide for herself instead of listening to family, cultural or society's expectations.*

I also thought back to a dinner I had at my mother's house where, in the end, a little compassion between my mother and I went a long way.

When I think about what I appreciate about my mother, it's her great hostess skills, sense of humor and strength to survive a divorce and start her own successful business. She taught me persistence, creative problem solving and how to be a modern-gourmet goddess cook by using a good tomato sauce with Italian herbs, simmered to perfection that comes in a jar from the super-market. (See recipe for modern-goddess-on-the-go lasagna in sixty minutes or less at the end of the chapter.) While we may have had differences over the years, as we've aged, we've come to a point of love and compassion for one another.

Three things are certain about my mother. One, she would do anything for her children; two, she will always love me; and three, one of the happiest days of her life will be when I, her thirty- forty- or fifty-something daughter, finally walks down the aisle.

I've often wondered why mothers are obsessed with marry-ing off their young? My Italian mother has been looking for a husband for me from the day I was born. I am told that even while she was recuperating from my birth, Mama was in the hospital nursery eyeing the newborn baby boys for any future son-in-law prospects.

The fact that her only daughter is still single is a reality my mother doesn't take lightly. Over the years she has been persistent and admirably creative in her attempts to get me to the altar. I remember a family boat trip where she proceeded to interview and collect resumes from the men on the nearby boats. Afterwards, I felt as if a flag had been hoisted that said: "single girl on board." While I was growing up, my mother always had my photo in her purse to show any unattached males she met during the day at the supermarket, hardware store or gas station. She was determined back then; I thought she might even start a support group called: Mothers Against Single Offspring (MASO) support, complete with T-shirts that said, "I have a single attractive daughter, do you have a son?"

In my twenties, my mother's real dream man for me was single, successful and Italian even though she did consider others. But now that I'm in my thirties, a man need only be single, employed, breathing and standing upright. But the other day, I think we had a semi-truce when she said, "I just want you to experience the love of a man, a home and family. Since you've waited this long to get married, you should hold out for the best one for you." *Hallelujah*, I thought to myself, the pressure is off. Until she added: "But don't wait too long because your biological clock is going ticky, ticky tock and I want some grandchildren."

For the record, I do look forward to being in a successful, loving marriage with a man who cherishes my feelings and me. Unfortunately, the relationship I thought would lead to marriage didn't work out because we were karmically incompatible. And until I meet the man I want to spend the rest of my life with my mother will have to wait. In order to do this, I gladly gave up my Italian Catholic guilt, fear and worry, which my grandmother brought over on "the boata from the olda country." And now, whenever a relative asks me why I'm not married yet, I smile and look them in the eye and say in a calm, spiritual voice: "When the time is right all things shall be revealed. Ommmmmmmm." Then I walk away chanting. This usually works and they never ask again. Except with one relative who thinks the reason I'm not married is because I don't eat red meat!

Dinners with my mother are always a memorable event. Once I brought a somewhat quiet date home for dinner with my family, and later he told me he hadn't experienced anything like that since Outward Bound, a wilderness survival course. Of course, when I had dinner at his family's house it was so quiet I could hear the clock ticking.

Last time I drove to my mother's house I was listening to the radio. A news story about world hunger made me think of my mother. She is a terrific cook/host who makes hundreds of meatballs and huge army pots of tomato sauce that she freezes in the event there are any last-minute dinner guests. She does make a difference in her world by making sure no one in the tri-county area is ever hungry. This was confirmed again, because when I arrived there were a few extra guests at the table—the UPS man, who I think my mother was trying to fix me up with, and Mario, the local gourmet butcher.

Dinner was a bit stressful. The gourmet butcher spent too much time talking about his loins. While the UPS man kept asking me out until I told him the only person I trust to hold my packages is the Fed Ex man.

I was happy for the break created when my spunky, four-foot, eleven-inch grandmother arrived. She affectionately put her hands on my cheeks and said "You're so skinny you looka like a piece of linguini. *Mangia, mangia.*" At that moment, my mother returned from the kitchen with a huge bowl of meatballs. "Mom, you know I don't eat beef." Before I could finish, my mother jumped in: "I know, but it's from Mario's shop." She persisted: "Come on, just try one, it won't kill you." "No thank you," I said. Well, she continued looking rejected. "I hope you're not turning into one of those vegetarians who eat nothing but Tofutti like your brother here."

My brother Carl and his girlfriend Leslie, who recently announced to my mother not that they were engaged but that they were vegetarians, looked at me, with compassionate smiles. Looking back, I should have known better than to refuse any of my ethnic foods, because to reject an Italian mother's food is to reject her.

My mother and I continued to debate a little more until things escalated with raised voices when Mario, the butcher, added that he thought vegetarianism was some sort of communist plot.

The dispute ended when my grandmother asserted her matriarchal power in a *Moonstruck* movie moment by hitting her hand on the table and saying in a loud voice, "ENOUGHA! When I grew up, you ate whatever was on the table. Women today have too many options. Work, travel, expensive dates and trips—in my day you were lucky to get an ice-cream cone!"

Everyone was silent for a moment then burst into laughter. Then my stepdad announced, "I'm also becoming a vegetarian.

But I'm doing it in stages and right now, I'm only eating things that eat vegetables—like cows. So please pass the meatballs!" Mario the butcher applauded.

This was followed by a compassionate mother-daughter moment when I realized how hard my mother aims to please. I reassured her that I still loved her and her meatballs. And she said she would find a recipe for turkey meatballs.

By dessert, I had survived the Italian Inquisition about my food intake and thought I might be experiencing a historic event—a dinner without any discussion of my marital status. But my mother cleverly got her message across once again—and this time it was through her cooking. For dessert, she served me a carrot cake and on the top was a bride statue . . . without a groom.

Inner-Wisdom Realization

"You can become your own nurturing mother." Regardless of what your mother-daughter relationship is or has been, mothering yourself as a loving mother does a precious child is essential to a modern-day goddess' well-being.

Modern-Day Goddess Contemplations

1. What do you appreciate about your mother?
2. What good qualities did you receive from your mother?
3. How has your mother influenced you to be like her or not like her?
4. Is there a way for you and your mother to be compassionate with one another? How can you communicate this?
5. How can you be a good mother to yourself? Or invoke the divine mother within?
6. If dinner with your family was an episode in a sitcom, what lines would get laughs?

What I Learned

Mothers are human and need compassion too.

Remember, you can listen to your mother's advice but that doesn't mean you have to use it.

Women have a choice about getting married.

Be who you are with your family, use gentle strength and humor whenever possible.

Never reject an Italian mother's food.

Look for humorous things your relatives say to write in journal as a way to lighten up family conversations that get intense.

Modern-Day-Goddess-on-the-Go Lasagna

(In sixty minutes or less)
(Preparation time: 30 minutes, Cooking time: 30 minutes)

This is the recipe my Italian mother taught me to cook before I went off to college—"so I could impress any male suitors." She said her mother, my grandmother, told her a woman would always have "male admirers" if she could cook a few things well. And before my grandmother married my grandfather, she always had admirers. Thus proving the old saying: "A way to a man's heart is through his stomach."

My mother and I have added a modern-day twist, which includes premade sauce from a jar and variations to the basic meat lasagna recipe. And since this lasagna is so delicious, there is no need to volunteer that the sauce came from the store; just smile and say thank you when they say it tastes great! This is also a great dish that you can make ahead, and freeze (without cooking) for a last-minute meal to treat yourself or share with your friends.

1 package lasagna noodles

1 garlic clove

1 medium onion, chopped

2 tablespoons olive oil

1 pound ground meat or vegetable variation (any combination of peppers, onions, carrots, mushrooms, zucchini, summer squash, eggplant or broccoli)

1 large jar of your favorite Italian tomato sauce

1 pound ricotta cheese

8 ounces mozzarella cheese, shredded, cubed or sliced

1 cup grated Parmesan cheese (the calorie conscious can use low-fat cheese)

Preheat oven to 350 degrees. Cook the lasagna noodles as per package instructions and set aside. While the noodles are cooking, lightly sauté the garlic and chopped onion in 2 tablespoons of olive oil for 2 to 3 minutes. Add the meat and cook for 4 to 6 minutes until lightly browned, or add the vegetable variation and sauté until vegetables are slightly tender.

Begin to assemble the lasagna by spreading several tablespoons of tomato sauce on the bottom of a shallow 2-quart pan. Cover the sauce with a layer of noodles, a layer of sauce, a layer of meat or vegetables, and a layer of spoonfuls of ricotta and mozzarella. Sprinkle the cheese layer with Parmesan cheese. Repeat the layers until the remaining ingredients are used, ending with a layer of mozzarella on top.

Cover the lasagna loosely with foil and bake in the oven for 30 to 35 minutes or until thoroughly heated and cheese has melted.

This recipe serves 4 to 6. Add some candles, relaxing music, a Caesar salad and amore (love for yourself, your friends or a male admirer). *Mangia* and enjoy!

with Mom

with Grandma

The Italian goddess sharing moments when I was young with my mother and her mother (my grandmother) and my favorite hats!

12

Goddess Self-Love: Dating Yourself

Dear Diary:

To me, Valentine's Day is a celebration of love that isn't just for lovers. It's a day to express love to yourself and others. So this year, I sent Valentine's Day cards to my mother, my grandmother, my grandfather, my single goddess friends and to myself.

For some lucky goddesses, Valentine's Day will consist of fragrant flowers, a heartfelt card and a day of love with a man who cherishes her for her inner spirit and emotions. Then there are the rest of us who will be solo. Perhaps you're like me and Mr. Right turned out to be karmically incompatible in a past life and in this life. Or maybe you're like a friend of mine, and your last five blind dates at Starbucks have only yielded a caffeine addiction.

Not to worry, there is a way to soothe your heart and soul—self-love.

My self-love quest led me to read *Creative Visualization* by Shakti Gawain. I soon discovered that even Oprah practices creative visualization and is quoted as saying: "I do believe and I have seen in my own life that creative visualization works."

In *Creative Visualization,* the author suggests visualizing exactly what you desire in your life. For example, if you would like to manifest a great date, you first visualize it and then treat yourself the way you would like to be treated. So that's exactly what I did. I created my own dream date.

First, I sent myself a dozen roses and acted surprised when they arrived. ("For me? Oh, you shouldn't have. Okay, I am worth it.") Then I called my answering machine from a pay phone and asked myself out for a Valentine's dinner—I was a little disappointed when I wasn't in. Next, I got all dressed up and went to a marvelous restaurant where I had a romantic and delicious meal. Even though I was self-conscious at first about being alone, the Italian waiters made sure I felt welcomed. The evening was wonderful because I felt like I had known myself my whole life! I told funny stories that made me laugh, cherished my feelings and intuitively knew I was karmically compatible. I even paid for the meal. At first a few people looked at me talking to myself, but then they seemed to assume I had too much wine.

At the end of the night, I was very gracious. I walked to my door and said goodnight without taking advantage of myself! Before I went to bed, I relaxed with a candlelit bath. As I fell asleep, I could have sworn I heard an angel whispering "I love you" in my ear and the tender touch of a celestial wing on my cheek. I felt like a goddess.

And the next day I called when I said I would! It was a perfect date. And the best part is, that afternoon in yoga class an attractive and kind man asked me out for dinner to the same restaurant. Even though there wasn't a spark between us, we had a nice time. Thank goddess for creative visualization!

Inner-Wisdom Realization

You can give yourself the precious gift of self-love by using creative visualization to help manifest a date or your heart's desire.

Modern-Day Goddess Contemplations

1. What special date can you plan for yourself?
2. What can you do for yourself to feel special?
3. How do you make yourself feel loved?
4. What would you like to visualize right now in your life?

What I Learned

Self-love comes first.

You can rely on yourself to create feelings of love.

You can date yourself and feel great.

Valentine's Day can be a wonderful day even if you are single.

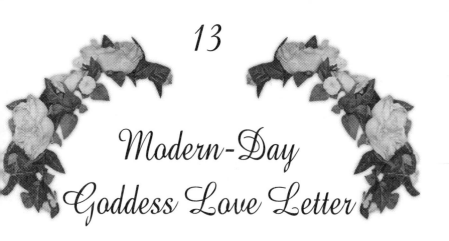

13

Modern-Day Goddess Love Letter

Dear Diary:

I just love to boost my spirits with a pure and simple love letter that I write and mail to my home. When it arrives days later, it's a sweet reminder in the midst of a busy day, that I do indeed love myself.

Last night, I read Louise Hay's <u>You Can Heal Your Life</u> which says self-love can help heal everything from relationships to finances to health. Louise also believes that self-love begins by never ever criticizing ourselves.

It's taken me years to understand that loving and approving of myself creates the self-esteem women need to become the goddesses we were put on this Earth to be.

Loving ourselves is also a lot healthier than being dependent on the love and approval of those around us. This could be why dogs, cats and house ferns are so popular—they love and approve of us no matter what.

I used to only apply self-love when I was scared or upset. Now, I make it a point to gently express love and encouragement for myself on an ongoing basis. Whether in my thoughts or in a card or letter, I like to express my appreciation for qualities I may take for granted and things I do, whether it's completing an errand, exercising, my sense of humor, speaking up for myself or taking the lemons life gives me and turning them into lemon chiffon pies.

Here are two love letter examples. One is a copy of a letter I sent to myself and the other is a fill-in-the-blank letter for you to create your own. Feel free to copy this one, fill in the following letter, or make up your own. It's an uplifting goddess gift to yourself, so enjoy!

Dear _____,

I just want you to know how much I love and accept you. To me, you are a beautiful, divine, courageous and cherished goddess. I'm writing this because I don't always take the time to stop and tell you how much I really appreciate you for all that you are. I'm also sorry if I've ever hurt you by not taking care of you, believing in you, criticizing you or scaring you with fearful thoughts. Please forgive me.

So I now want to acknowledge and recognize you for just how amazing you really are. Your sensitivity, spirituality, creativity, sense of humor, compassion and willingness to create an authentic life are just a few of the wonderful things I love about you.

When I think of your heart, I marvel at all your love and generosity. When I think of your mind, I am awed at your wisdom and intuition. When I think of your soul, I know I am with an angel goddess.

Thank you for all that you are, for all that you do and for all that you bring to the world by just being you.

I cherish our life together and the way you love and take care of me. My life, the life of others, and the world are a better place because of you. And, I feel blessed to be together forever!

I love you!

Love, Me

Dear _____,

I just want you to know how much I love and accept you.

You are _____. [List five qualities you like about yourself. For example, smart, beautiful, kind, a great friend, great yard-sale price negotiator.]

I'm also sorry if I've ever hurt you by not taking care of you, believing in you, criticizing you or scaring you with fearful thoughts. And I'm sorry if I said I told you so about dating that last guy. But please forgive me and remember to listen to me next time.

I love you and your _____.
[List five physical attributes: warm smile, sparkling eyes, laughter, belly button.]

I love that you are _____.
[List spiritual qualities: Divine, centered, spiritual, beautiful inside and out, a yoga addict.]

I love and cherish you with all of my heart. And you can always count on me always being there for you throughout your life.

Thank you for your love, taking care of me and creating a wonderful life.

I love you!

Love, Me XXXXOOOOO

Inner-Wisdom Realization

You can experience a greater sense of self-worth by nurturing and acknowledging yourself with a simple love letter.

Modern-Day Goddess Contemplations

1. How would it feel to receive a love letter from yourself?
2. What would you say in your love letter?
3. When can you fit in time to write yourself a love letter?

What I Learned

Writing a love letter is a wonderful way to have a love affair with yourself.

Acknowledging and appreciating yourself is nurturing.

You don't have to wait for someone else to write you a love letter, you can do it for yourself.

Enjoying a love letter to myself!

Photo by Sally Franz.

14

Conscious Male Wanted

Dear Diary:

Please bring me a man who is in touch with his feminine side, and that doesn't mean he calls his mother three times a day.

The definition of a conscious male (CM) used to be a man who did not return drunk after a night out with the guys, who put the toilet seat down and stayed awake for at least a minute and a half after having sex. But now, as we women work on being goddesses who are in touch with our inner beauty, inner peace and inner thighs, we are raising the standards for the millennium male. Today, women are trying all sorts of enlightenment activities to heal their feminine self. Gone are our mothers' days of Tupperware parties and quilting. Modern-day goddesses are exploring therapy, reiki and meditating instead of medicating. To many goddesses, personal growth work is an equal-opportunity experience.

Which means, a man saying he is sorry with flowers and a card alone won't cut it anymore. Now we also want to hear that he knows his inner child was acting out of fear and he won't do it again.

My girlfriend Moonbeam and I were discussing where conscious males come from. Luckily, some men were given a CM gene at birth. Others were dragged by the pain of life onto the CM path, as they searched for damage-control techniques for failed relationships that propelled them into therapy or started them reading one of the gazillion self-help books women have given them over the past ten years.

As a modern-day goddess I am a conscious male appreciator. Why? Because a conscious male has the basics such as love, trust, respect, honesty, communication, the ability to keep his word and the capacity to make us laugh when our hormones dip so low that even we don't want to be around ourselves. (Not to worry—smart, rich and attractive are still pluses, but I have learned from experience that these things don't always equal a man of integrity.)

So how does a goddess locate a conscious male? Forget about looking for him in a bar. This is a breeding ground for a majority of men who like to go unconscious with alcohol. Moonbeam and I have decided a yoga class, personal-growth seminar, health-food store, local meditation center, cultural event or chiropractor's office are much better places.

Another way to meet a conscious male is to ask a girlfriend who is married to one to introduce you to her husband's fellow CM tribe members. (CMs like to hang out in groups.) You can also ask an unavailable, married CM to introduce you to his friends. So, that's just what I did today when I went to visit my acupuncturist. While the needles were sticking out from my body, I asked him if he knew any heartfelt and successful CMs I could meet. He said yes, and he would work on a few introductions.

Moonbeam and I decided it could be hard work locating a CM, but the payoff is a man who will cherish us as the beautiful, divine, heartfelt, sexy and smart goddesses we are. And this will create the added bonus of mutual appreciation for each other that will open the door to a divine relationship and blissful lovemaking!

Below is a quiz I made up for myself, Moonbeam and my other girlfriends, to help determine whether we have found a true CM male and not some clever man who only pretends to speak in CM lingo to pick up goddesses!

1. Your CM candidate is in a yoga class and afterwards he:
   a. Stays an extra ten minutes to savor his inner peace.
   b. Tries to get the phone numbers of several women who he watched intensely as they did an arching back pose.
   c. Asks the instructor how he can get a black belt in yoga.

2. Your CM candidate thinks a higher power is:
   a. An all-knowing source that you can connect with to guide you.
   b. Timothy Leary.
   c. Bill Gates.

3. You're at a party and the hostess serves a CM candidate
   a tofu cube, and he:
   a. Tries one out of curiosity.
   b. Declines because he is aware he is tofu intolerant.
   c. Says, "Alright, Jell-O shots! Let's party!"

4. Your CM candidate thinks a men's group is a place to:
   a. Speak and feel from your heart and not your head.
   b. Play weekly poker.
   c. Have a bachelor party with strippers.

5. Your CM candidate thinks Feng Shui is:
   a. The Chinese art of furniture placement and harmony.
   b. An athlete's foot spray—"Feng Shui away!"
   c. A 1970's song—"Everybody Was Feng Shui Fighting."

6. Your CM candidate regards Tantric Sex as:
   a. A conscious way of communicating and making love
      with your partner.
   b. A drink with peach Schnapps in it.
   c. A type of sex where you throw a tantrum if you don't
      have multiple orgasms.

7. Your CM candidate thinks being authentic means:
   a. Telling the truth with integrity.
   b. Wearing cotton and not polyester.
   c. Blurting out everything that pops into his head, like:
      "Wow, you look fat in those pants."

8. Your CM candidate regards abundance as:
   a. Prosperity in all areas of your life.
   b. A Bun Dance where you shake your booty on the
      dance floor.

c. Wads of cash, a slender babe, a thick prime rib steak and a fat cigar.

9. Your CM candidate's idea of being committed is:
   a. Keeping promises and having integrity.
   b. Entering a mental institution.
   c. Being punctual for your golf tee-time.

10. Your CM candidate regards marriage as:
    a. The blissful union of two soul mates.
    b. Something to be feared.
    c. A merger deal.

If you were able to answer "A" to all of these questions, congratulations! You may have found a conscious male. Just remember to check him out for the basics, such as love, trust, respect, honesty, communication, the ability to keep his word and a capacity to make you laugh when life isn't so funny. If you picked more B's and C's than A's, it's time to raise the standards of what type of man you would like to spend your goddess life with. Remember, no settling! A woman who has put the time and effort into learning to be a goddess of joy and love is worthy of a conscious male.

Inner-Wisdom Realization

You deserve a kind and conscious male who loves, cares, cherishes, understands and respects you for the goddess that you are.

Modern-Day Contemplations

1. What conscious male qualities would you like to have in a mate?
2. If you are in a relationship, does your current partner have these qualities?
3. If you are single, who can you ask and where can you go in your area to meet conscious males?
4. What qualities do you have that would be attractive to a mate?

What I Learned

Seek out a good quality man who will love and cherish you and your feelings.

It's better to be single than to settle for a man who will age you quicker than a lack of estrogen.

Look for inner qualities instead of only examining the external material things.

Conscious males hang out in tribes; find a way to meet a brave.

When you do find a conscious male, take your time getting to know him. If he's worth it, he won't rush you into anything you're not ready for.

15

Divine Dating

Dear Diary:

I've come to realize that meeting that special someone may be like a scene in a movie—or maybe not. Especially when a relationship turns out not to be "the one." But each relationship can be viewed as a stepping stone that gives you the lessons you need to prepare for your soul mate.

I have always been a romantic comedy film fan and today in a screenwriting workshop, I learned if you want to write a romantic comedy, there has to be a "cute meet"— the moment where the man and woman meet. My two favorite celestial films with "cute meets" both take place in heaven. Timothy Hutton and Kelly McGillis meet there in <u>Made in Heaven</u> and so do Meryl Steep and Albert Brooks in <u>Defending Your Life.</u>

Being an eternal romantic, I've always wanted my own "cute meet" and one day God, the ultimate director and *scriptwriter delivered it to me—not in heaven but in church. I was so moved, I want to share it with everyone. So here is how I met a wonderful and spiritual man that felt like a scene from a romantic movie.*

A UNITY CHURCH

CINDY, a petite, attractive, slender brunette in her late thirties with sparkling green eyes and a radiant smile is visiting Unity, a nondenominational spiritual church. She is wearing a cast on her right arm. Cindy has come to Unity to seek comfort, faith and love.

The USHER, a bubbling older woman in her sixties, greets Cindy.

> USHER
>
> Welcome, I haven't seen you here before.

> CINDY
>
> I'm new and I thought this might be the place to make a direct call to God. I tried e-mailing him but his Website, *God.com*, was busy.

> USHER
>
> Well, you're at the right place—we even have special dial-direct Sunday rates. The service will be starting soon. Here, let me put this guest ribbon on you, so people can welcome you with a hug. I should tell you ahead of time that we're a pretty touchy, feely church.

> CINDY
>
> Thanks. I could use some major hug therapy.

Cindy slides into her seat. A FEMALE VOCALIST melodizes a worship song. Cindy bows down to pray. EDDY and PATTY enter—a talented husband and wife co-minister team.

Always personable, they are holding hands and smiling as they walk down the aisle to the front of the church.

> EDDY
>
> Today's lesson is about the power of believing. For this we need a crack in the consciousness—so we can believe and have faith that a miracle is possible.

A few pews behind Cindy is DAVID. He is handsome, physically fit, with sun-kissed blonde hair, blue eyes and a smile that lights up a room.

DAVID notices Cindy and smiles to himself as she turns toward the sermon.

> CINDY
> (Voice-Over)
>
> Let's see, I have a crack in my wrist from getting on the motorcycle, a crack in my heart from the driver and a crack in my bank account from him not having any insurance.

> EDDY
>
> Now, I want everyone to think about their prayer request. And please allow a crack in your consciousness to believe that God wants you to have abundance.

> CINDY
> (Voice-Over)
>
> Okay, God. Please help me, I surrender my life to you. It's obvious I don't know what I'm doing. Please heal my wrist, my life, make me feel like a goddess and bring me my soul mate: a spiritually evolved male who is in touch with his feminine side but doesn't have more shoes than me.

David is asked to help pass the collection basket. All the volunteers are walking toward the front as Cindy spots David.

CINDY
(Voice-Over)

Ooooh, he looks divine. Please, please God, let him come to my pew—oh, here he comes. Oh yes, thank-you Jesus! (BEAT) Ohh, I feel flushed. Maybe I'm overreacting a bit. Now, calm down, honey.

At that moment an elder gentleman drops the collection basket in the front row. Bills fall in the aisle next to Cindy. David saves the elder man from embarrassment by picking up the money.

Cindy and David's eyes meet as he passes the collection basket her way. They both smile at each other.

CINDY
(Voice-Over)

Oh, how nice of him to help that older man. He must be a kind person.

Eddy begins the prosperity blessing.

EDDY

" . . . Divine love through me, blesses and multiplies all that I am, all that I have, all that I give and all that I receive, and I send it forth with my blessings and my love." Thank you for joining us, coffee will be served outside.

CINDY exits and walks down the aisle.

CINDY
(Voice-Over)

Okay, God, you've got to arrange the details of this meeting. You know I'm not so great with the details. Please, God, please, if you do I promise to always listen to you. Thank you. [PAUSE] Breathe and remember—I am a beautiful and divine goddess.

David catches her eye as he is leaving the pew.

DAVID

Hi, my name is David.
(spotting her guest badge)
Welcome.

David extends his arms for a hug.

CINDY

Hi. I'm Cindy.

Cindy, mesmerized, walks into David's arms, and their hug lasts longer than usual.

EFFECTS: A flash frame of white light reveals David's arms as big angel wings wrapping around Cindy.

An ELDERLY COUPLE in their seventies walk by and take a double look. Inspired by their hug, the elderly gentleman hugs his wife.

ELDERLY MAN

Oooh, that sure looks like a heavenly hug. Come here honey, I want one.

CUT BACK TO: Cindy and David in an embrace. Cindy is melting in David's arms and looking up at the heavens.

CINDY

Thank you, God, thank you!

CUT TO: A church choir singing Halleluiah.

AT THE BEACH several months later. David and Cindy are enjoying a romantic picnic by the sea.

CINDY

Honey, when after our first heavenly hug did you know you wanted to be with me?

DAVID

The moment we hugged. It happened just like they say in my favorite country song by Kenny Chesney, "You Had Me from Hello."

Cindy and David's hearts melt as they kiss and embrace while the sun sets in the background.

Inner-Wisdom Realization

You can create divine dating and other romantic miracles by asking God for help!

Modern-Day Goddess Contemplations

1. What are your favorite "cute meets" in a movie? How would you write your own "cute meet" in real life?
2. What feelings would a divine relationship give you?
3. Have you ever invited the divine into your personal relationships? What happened?
4. What would your divine dating scene be like?

What I Learned

Believe you deserve to be loved.

If you want to find a spiritual mate, go to spiritual places.

Love can happen when you least expect it.

Don't be afraid to give someone a hug.

Divine dating can happen to you.

16

Love, Modern-Day Goddess Style

Dear Diary:

I've learned that once you've "man"ifested your man, there will always be lessons to learn about love. Like, the most important relationship is the one with yourself. If you can love and accept who you are, then you will be able to love and accept your mate.

Or that we need to forgive our parents and family members who did the best they could given their understanding and circumstances. If we don't, the universe often brings us a mate with qualities we haven't forgiven a family member for yet.

The other day, I looked back at my dating history and realized I had dated men with traits from almost every one of my family members, except our dog, Snoopy. I knew I was complete when I met a soul mate, and it felt like puppy love.

s the relationships between men and women evolve toward a higher love, I feel so lucky to learn relationship principles and techniques my parents and grandparents never had a chance to learn. Especially since the only advice I received growing up was: "Don't go to bed angry," from my Italian grandfather; "Don't go to bed hungry," from my Italian grandmother; and "Marry as soon as possible," from my Italian mother.

I've read lots of books on love and relationships, taken love workshops and experienced my share of heartbreaks and loving moments.

I once attended a workshop called Marriage God's Way given by two Santa Barbara pastors Gary Rieben and Bracy Ball. They said while there are hundreds of relationship techniques—the basic principles stay the same.

They also suggested using the passage from 1 Corinthians 13:47 as a model to see how you are doing in your relationship:

> "*Love is patient, love is kind, and is not jealous; love does not brag and is not arrogant, does not act unbecomingly, it does not seek its own, it's not provoked, does not take into account a wrong suffered, does not rejoice in unrighteousness, but rejoices with the truth; bears all things, believes all things, hopes all things, endures all things.*"

From this, I've learned what contributes to a fabulous relationship.

Along with my modern-day-goddess-on-the-go lasagna recipe, here's a recipe to feed your soul.

A Modern-Day Goddess Loving Relationship Recipe

Take two soul mates. Then combine the remaining ingredients below according to taste. Mix daily with a higher power.

Lots of love	Celebrating
Unconditional love	Laughter
Self-love	Joy
Kindness	Sensitivity
Compassion	Hugs, kisses, cuddling
Commitment	Romance
Honesty	Quiet time
Acceptance	Letting go of fear
Sense of humor	Positive, abundant thinking
Good communication	Sharing
Friendship	Forgiveness
Patience	Another successfully married
Passion	couple as a role model
A willingness to grow	A therapist when needed
Knowledge of your inner-self	A few self-help books on
Appreciation	romance and love
Conscious truth-telling	Some vacation time

Let simmer for the rest of your life and enjoy. This recipe yields unlimited scrumptious servings for loving relationship success.

Inner-Wisdom Realization

Once you've found your mate, you have the power to increase your chances for lasting bliss by applying the principles for a successful relationship.

Modern-Day Goddess Contemplations

1. How can you practice more kindness and compassion with your beloved?
2. What do you appreciate and cherish about your mate?
3. If you are single, what would your daily life be like with your mate?
4. If you are a couple, what can you do to learn ways to create a strong foundation of love through counseling, books, tapes or workshops?

What I've Learned

Let go, let God.

You must love yourself first to love another.

Our partners can be mirrors of our thought patterns.

Intimacy is a premium today, and you have to work at your love relationship just like everything else.

It is a blessing to find a man who is willing to do the emotional work with you.

Couples therapy and books can help you get the right tools to create a long-lasting relationship together.

A few sessions of premarital counseling before getting married can help a great deal.

Planning romance and loving gestures are fun and healing for both parties.

PART IV:

Modern-Day Goddess Explorations

17

A Chakra-Balancing Massage

Dear Diary:

Today I balanced my tires, my diet and my chakras for under one hundred dollars. It really helped because I was still feeling some stress in my body one year later from the motorcycle accident—an event that definitely shocked my chakras. I was craving some major self-nurturing but a trip to Hawaii was on my fantasy wish list only and not in my bank account. So, today I decided the next best thing would be a chakra-balancing massage at Cherubs.

Cherubs is a magical aromatherapy, gift and garden shop nestled against the mountains in the picturesque town of Ojai, California. Outside the shop, angel fountains and statues are lined up on the patio as if a mystical convention was in session. As I approached the store, the sweet aromatherapy scent of rose oil wafted out the door, enticing me to enter. Inside, I discovered that angels manifest in many forms. There were angel frames, books, magnets and even a set of angel wings you could call your own.

The owner, Sherrie Dawkins, resembled an angel with her serene smile. Her name was easy to recall because it wasn't a long spiritual name I couldn't pronounce or never forget, like the really creative name of my Hindu plumber, "Soon To Be Flushing Water."

Sherrie, a certified massage therapist, showed me a brochure on the different types of massages. I found myself intrigued by the chakra-balancing massage that she described as "absolutely euphoric! Eighty dollars." Euphoria for only eighty dollars? I was sold. Plus, eighty dollars was much cheaper than a plane ticket to Maui. I wondered if a chakra balancing for the lower half of my body was only forty dollars.

"So what exactly is a chakra?" I asked Sherrie.

"They are the seven energy centers of the body that have a physical and emotional connection," she answered.

"What about my third-eye chakra? Would you be able to tell me if it needs glasses?" I joked.

"We can definitely take a look and see what we find," she chuckled.

Sherrie explained that her chakra-balancing massage was unique because eight to fifteen precious oils from Europe were specifically blended for each chakra. Aromatherapy can have a positive effect on moods, emotions, hormones and even your sex drive. She also said that massage can transport a person to a state of total relaxation. *Aaah yes, total relaxation,* I thought, *like the way a goddess feels after divine lovemaking.*

The massage took place in a tranquil room with a shelf of colorful aromatherapy bottles, lit candles and a divine cherub child angel hanging on the wall who looked happy to see me. Or at least, the angel pretended it was happy to see me. I floated into heaven when Sherrie began applying certain scents to different chakra areas using oils like rose, sandalwood and mugwort.

Mugwort? I decided to not ask any questions.

What was fascinating were her insights as she performed the massage. The root/base chakra and tailbone, which corresponds to the family of origin, and my navel chakra/lower back area, which related to my finances, were definitely tight. *How accurate*, I thought. I was a bit stressed over finances—so this must be the checkbook-balancing chakra. And as for my family chakra, I was going to visit my Italian mother in Connecticut for a few days.

Sherrie said my heart chakra was totally opened, which I felt was true since I was happy with my love life, and I had learned to love myself by being willing to say I was sorry after I had a fight with my inner-self. Sherrie also said my third eye, which corresponds to the spiritual center, was totally open like that of a yogi or spiritual teacher. (She offered me a turban, but I declined since they were extra.) She was also happy to report that my third eye did not need glasses. As for my career, which corresponded to the throat chakra, I was doing the right work—but many more good things were to occur in the future.

The massage, the insights and the sweet scents of the oils created a beautiful healing experience that levitated me off the table and back into my car for the drive back to Santa

Barbara. On the way, the traffic slowed down. Instead of stressing, I felt like a balanced goddess. To relax, I closed my eyes for a few moments and inhaled the scents that still lingered on my body. I found myself transported to a beautiful flower and herb garden for a short time . . . at least until the car behind me beeped its horn, and I realized I was now the reason for a tangled twenty-car traffic jam!

Inner-Wisdom Realization

You can release stress, lighten up and feel a sense of well-being with aromatherapy and massage.

Modern-Day Goddess Contemplations

1. Have you ever experienced a massage that totally relaxed you?
2. Have you ever had an aromatherapy massage?
3. How can you incorporate an aromatherapy experience into your life?

What I Learned

Our bodies store emotions that can be released during massage. Aromatherapy is an affordable bliss you can experience with or without massage, scented candles, bubble bath, lotions, oil and diffuser.

When your chakras are balanced, your body, mind and spirit feel balanced.

Have someone drive you home from a massage for added relaxation.

18

Feng Shui Fun

Dear Diary:

Today I really appreciated living in a spiritual hot spot like Santa Barbara. I sought out some celestial fun with Feng Shui, and I found it amusing that no one here thought twice when I said: "I have to go now because I have an appointment with my Feng Shui consultant."

The first time I heard the word *Feng Shui* I thought it was a gourmet mushroom. But I soon discovered it wasn't a food item at all. Feng Shui is an ancient Chinese system used to create harmony in your living environment and keep the "chi" or life force energy flowing. When applied, it can enhance abundance in many areas of your life. Basically, with Feng Shui you can redesign your whole life by rearranging your stuff.

I first became intrigued with Feng Shui after hearing Yuki Ming, a successful Feng Shui consultant, speak at a women's networking luncheon. Yuki talked enthusiastically about the success, prosperity and love her clients were creating with Feng Shui. Her consultation fee: $125 an hour.

Before spending that kind of money, I decided to learn more about Feng Shui and see if I could do it myself. So, I skimmed a few books on the topic at my local spiritual bookstore. Many of the books were filled with victory stories of people using Feng Shui to manifest boatloads of cash, yachts, palaces for homes, fancy cars, soul mates, better health, harmonious family relations, less stress at work, job promotions and even new wardrobes.

There were also lots of diagrams on how to rearrange your furniture for optimal Feng Shui—something my mother used to do at 2:00 A.M. when she couldn't sleep. Obviously, Mom was onto something.

One Feng Shui book talked about the importance of placing your bed in various positions such as facing southeast, north, etc. to increase everything from health to fame. *They should include a compass with this book,* I thought. Body positions were not mentioned in any Feng Shui books but *were* discussed in detail in the nearby Tantra sex manuals. For this you don't need a compass, but a willing love partner, which is definitely something they don't sell at a hardware store.

Another book said to make certain all of your shoes were facing the same way for a clear direction in your career, and I suspect for walking. No instructions were given if they should face north, south, east or be hung on the ceiling.

There was also information on determining the numerology

of you and your home. Perhaps you are a "five" living in a "two" house—does that make you a lucky seven? But what if you are a zero living in a zero house? Do you then not even exist?

In Feng Shui, there is also a Bagua map. This octagonal-shaped map relates to the special areas of your life such as relationships and love, prosperity, wisdom and knowledge, fame and reputation, career and life path, creativity and children, helpful people and travel, family and health. The bagua is used to determine which room and corners of your home correspond to each area of your life exam.

The different schools and philosophies of Feng Shui confused me even further on how I would specifically implement it into my life. By the time I was done reading, my mind was filled with too many details about maps, compasses and directions—things that can overwhelm a directionally challenged goddess like myself.

I was also worried that I might place the wrong item in the wrong "life area" and cause more damage than good. So, I sat down for a moment in the bookstore among the chimes, cards and crystals, took a deep breath and contemplated my next step. Obviously, it was time to call in a professional. I reached into my purse, found my cell phone and dialed Yuki's number.

Luckily, she was home. Yuki assured me she could help. When I learned she also had an interior-design background, I thought that at the very least I would get a few decorating tips. She said our hour-and-a-half consultation would include a look at my place and discussions about what I wanted to enhance in my life.

To prepare, I returned home after a stop at the ATM machine, and as many women before me have been known to tidy up the house before the maid arrives, I cleaned the entire house for Yuki. As I vacuumed, I mused how modern-day-goddess living now involved paying a consultant to analyze your life by inspecting your house. While I know I have all the answers within me, I do like to try new things to see whether or not they can contribute to creating a more sacred and abundant life for me. There are no guarantees, but I figured it couldn't hurt.

Yuki arrived the next day at the appointed time toting a Bagua map and wearing a Kimono jacket. She was personable and professional. Since she didn't look Asian, I asked her if Yuki Ming was her real name. She said: "No, I'm really Irish, and my birth name is Kelly O'Flannagan. But I chose the name Yuki because I enjoy the Asian culture, which gave birth to Feng Shui, my profession. I also love the Oriental traditions, which is why I wear Japanese kimonos." I wondered if my consultation might include a Japanese tea ceremony.

Yuki then began to explain a few Feng Shui principles. "In Feng Shui, clutter is bad. It not only blocks the chi, which is the universal life force, but it also clutters the mind," Yuki said, while looking around my living room for any clutter.

"I see you don't have any clutter and your place is very clean. That's good," she said.

"Thanks," I answered, feeling glad I cleaned before she arrived but also a bit guilty that I deceived her about how I really lived.

"Good chi can also escape. How is your career doing?"

"Okay," I answered. "But I'm in search of a good publisher for my book."

"Hmmm. I thought so," Yuki said. "You see this sliding glass door? It's positioned so the chi rushes out when you open up the front door."

"Well, I don't have any plans to move my front door. Plus that's quite expensive," I answered.

"Luckily, you don't have to. A simple crystal will correct that. Crystals, fountains, chimes, plants, candles are some of the known 'cures' for Feng Shui ailment."

"Good, a crystal is a lot cheaper than taking a sledge-hammer to the walls. Besides, the landlord wouldn't like it if I started renovating the building without a permit," I said.

"Exactly. How is your health?" she asked.

"Well, I have a sensitive stomach, and I'm wheat gluten intolerant," I answered, feeling like I was in the midst of a doctor's office exam.

"It sounds like your health area could use some help," she answered. "Let's take a look at your bedroom."

"Hmmm," Yuki said. "Just what I thought. This overstuffed closet is your health and family corner." *Busted*, I thought. *Now she knows I really do have clutter.* "Clear out as much as possible and put up a photo of a healthy, strong woman. It will help you heal quicker," Yuki instructed.

She walked over to another corner. "I bet your romantic life isn't so great, either, because there is a trash can in your love corner."

"That would explain a lot of things about my last rela-tionship—and why the garbage man winked at me the other day," I said.

"Get rid of the trash right away. Add some pink candles, a photo of a couple in love, and a vase of roses." Yuki said with urgency.

"Your skills and knowledge area is a little cluttered. If you clear it away this would make a nice meditation space. You can put some candles, a crystal and a photo of your meditation master," Yuki said.

"Okay," I replied, furiously taking notes.

We continued to walk around with the Bagua map, inspecting the different corners and rooms of the apartment in search of blocked or runaway chi. Yuki explained that the Bagua map could also be applied to offices, cars, even your desk to determine the corresponding Feng Shui corners of love, wealth, etc. "What about a saltine?" I asked. "I could be nibbling away at the wealth corner and not know it." Yuki assured me that I didn't have to take Feng Shui to the extreme, and I could eat in harmony.

"Let's take a look at your wealth corner," Yuki said. "Hmm. Your wealth corner is a barren table with a box of bills. How are your finances?" Yuki said.

"Not great. I could use more, especially for the basics such as rent, food, gas and a better car." I answered, feeling a bit down.

Yuki noticed my sad expression. "Don't worry. Just add some red and purple flowers, a light purple tablecloth, and a fountain for prosperity and see what happens. "

"Okay," I said, jotting down some more notes. My list of items to buy or find was growing. I asked myself: *I wonder when an item isn't considered clutter. Perhaps when it's not in a group?*

"Let's also look at your bathroom, where lots of chi can escape," Yuki said. "Just what I thought. Keep the drains closed and especially the toilet seat cover. Otherwise your chi, or abundance, will go down the drain and get flushed down the toilet."

"Aha, Yuki," I said. "This toilet seat thing is something

women have known intuitively their whole lives, when they say: "Please, put the seat down."

Yuki chuckled. As we continued surveying my stuff, she suggested photos of helpful people on my bookcase, which was my helpful people and travel corner; a live plant and chimes in my creativity and children's corner, which also represented my inner child; and a red ribbon in my fame and reputation corner.

I looked down at my list, which now had over twenty items to do or buy. I told Yuki I was feeling a bit down again from realizing there were so many areas of my life that needed help. She said it was only temporary, and if I did what she suggested, my chi—the good energy—would become unblocked and bring me good fortune in each area of my life.

She said I could also use the power of visualization to increase my abundance by creating a vision board with images cut out from magazines of what I wanted to manifest in all areas of my life.

Our session ended. I said good-bye and flopped onto my bed to process everything. After a thirty-minute meditation, I felt the urge to begin my Feng Shui renovation by cutting out magazine pictures of health, wealth, love and abundance.

I followed Yuki's suggestions and added a few of my own. In my helpful people and travel corner, I decided to include a picture of a woman traveling with ease and a photo of Oprah. In my wealth corner, I placed several fake million-dollar bills and a fountain. In my love corner, I put a rose quartz crystal, a list of what I wanted specifically in a mate, and a framed copy of Corinthians love message: "Love is patient, Love is kind. . . . Love endures all things." In my family corner, a photo of my family looking happy was placed. I had to draw smiles on some of their faces. In my wisdom and knowledge corner, I created a wonderful meditation space that I now look forward to sitting in each day.

Next, I cleaned out my closet and tossed ten bags filled with no-longer-needed items, such as clothes, papers, books, etc. The next weekend, I had a yard sale for any other items I could no longer use. As I let go of stuff, I chanted the affirmation: "Out with the old and in with the new."

In my career corner, I designed a prototype cover for my book with a photo of me looking confident and successful. In my fame corner, I put a fake Emmy award statue I would like to win for my successful TV show. I added crystals where needed, wind chimes for effect, burned incense and kept the toilet seat down.

Each day for a week, I waited for things to change. Nothing happened.

While I read that Feng Shui is only ten percent of the manifestation process, and intention, prayer, visualization and self-effort the remaining, I began to get a bit disheartened. As I looked around my room, I wondered if I had just exchanged old clutter for new clutter. My yard sale had yielded $125.19 while my new Feng Shui items cost $124.99. I was only ahead by twenty cents. I immediately turned on the fountain in my wealth corner. Even though nothing had manifested yet, my space did feel more sacred and relaxing, which made me feel more focused and uplifted. And I was drawn to more prayer and meditation, which created more peace of mind and creativity.

The night before my birthday, I prayed for two hours and surrendered my life to God to manifest the divine plan of my life. It had become obvious to me that when I tried to work things out on my own, they didn't manifest very well. I said: "Okay, God, I need some help here. If you want me to be the author of this book, then I need you to show me the way by providing a good publisher, enough money to live on and—as long as I'm making requests—a wonderful mate would be nice, too."

Something worked. The next day on my birthday, I received the best present of all: a message on my answering machine praising my book and offering me a book contract.

Since then, my health has improved, and I found I could actually get myself up early to go to the gym on several mornings and then come back and meditate. It's the perfect yin/yang workout that makes me feel balanced. I had a pleasant trip with my family and positive talks with my relatives. My life is constantly filled with lots of helpful people, and I've been able to spend some time watching Oprah and discovering lots of valuable advice.

The best part of all—within two weeks, my girlfriend and I went to our local Unity church where I met a wonderful, attractive and spiritual man.

Running full speed ahead, for an entire month, I played a subliminal prosperity tape and kept my fountain running on high. (I eventually had to keep it on low since the sound of the water had me forever running to the bathroom.) Within a month, I received a public-speaking opportunity and a large amount of unexpected cash that allowed me to get a great car.

I now use Feng Shui to create an optimal environment. Each day I look at my vision board of my life and say, "This or something better now manifests." When I am negotiating a writing project, a speaking opportunity, media appearance or doing something creative and I want to be Feng Shui aligned, I'll first make sure there isn't any clutter in the appropriate areas, and then play my subliminal tape with ocean waves for prosperity or peak performance. To increase the good chi, Yuki says to place a fresh flower with an intention of increasing abundance in the appropriate life corner. If an important call comes in unexpectedly and I want some extra grace, I'll put them on hold, say a quick prayer that whatever manifests is for my higher good, check to see if my fountain and aromatherapy diffuser are turned on, and if needed, move to my career corner. Also, when I speak to my sweetheart on the phone, I look at my love images and talk from my love corner. I'm not saying there are any guarantees, but I figure it can't hurt.

Inner-Wisdom Realization

You can create more harmony in your life by eliminating clutter and turning your environment into a sacred space.

Modern-Day Goddess Contemplations

1. How could a Feng Shui consultant help you?
2. Do you feel your living environment is harmonious and sacred?
3. What areas of your life would you like to work on?
4. Is there any clutter that you can clear out?
5. Do you have a sacred space where you can meditate?

What I Learned

A cluttered life is a cluttered mind.

A harmonious living environment contributes to success, inner peace and a sense of well-being.

Don't attempt Feng Shui on your own.

Find an experienced and successful Feng Shui consultant through a referral.

A vision board, meditation and prayer can increase your manifestation powers.

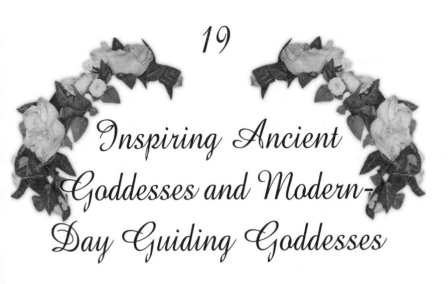

19

Inspiring Ancient Goddesses and Modern-Day Guiding Goddesses

Dear Diary:

Last night, I dreamt about being an ancient goddess of mirth in Egypt. I was surrounded by handsome warriors and hanging out with Cleopatra, laughing and discussing meditation, personal growth and makeup. Cleo hadn't heard of antioxidant creams yet, but she did show me how to crush berries for lipstick and use charcoal for eyeliner. Our fun was interrupted when a battle broke out and she had to give instructions to the men.

In the dream, someone handed me a sword for protection. I successfully fought off the enemies like I was Xena, The Warrior Princess, and woke up triumphant, with the taste of wild berries on my lips. I was relieved when I found myself safe in bed surrounded by my goddess books, cards and amulets. I fell back asleep wondering how many other women dream of goddesses?

he very word *goddess* conjures up images of heavenly women from ancient times dressed in flowing gowns with headdresses. For centuries, goddesses have been idolized for traits such as beauty, strength, power and wisdom.

While there are hundreds of goddesses, here are some ancient goddesses with characteristics I have found inspiring. As you read them, think about any attributes they have that you find appealing and how you could incorporate them into your daily living.

Hanging out with some goddesses at one of my favorite museums, the Art Institute of Chicago.

Photo by Beverly Kirkhart.

ARTEMIS

Greek Goddess of the Hunt and the Moon

The archer, protector of women,
children and animals

A woman who can seek her own
goals on her own terrain

ARTEMIS TRAITS:

Independent feminine spirit

Competent

Huntress

Intense concentration

Goal-focused

Disciplined

Lover of nature

The following goddesses are adapted from several sources: *Goddesses in Every Woman* by Jean Shinoda Bolen, M.D., *The Goddesses' Mirror* by David Kinsley, *The Goddess Oracle* by Amy Marashinsky and *The Goddess Card Pack* by Juni Parkhurst. (See Book and Resources list for papers and additional information.)

APHRODITE

The Greek goddess of love and beauty

Rules a woman's enjoyment of love,
beauty, sexuality and sensuality

Drives a woman toward both
creativity and procreativity

Has intense, passionate involvement with
creative work, as if it's a lover

Aphrodite, known as Venus to the Romans,
is portrayed on the half-shell in Botticelli's
"The Birth of Venus"

APHRODITE TRAITS:

Attractive

Enchanting

Romantic

Sensual

Loving oneself, others and life

Full of laughter

Warm

A love of luxury, comfort and beauty

Inspirational

Kind

ATHENA

Greek goddess of culture and civilization

A stately, beautiful warrior-goddess

Guardian of the city of Athens,
associated with the arts and war

A goddess to have on your side if
you need to go to battle

ATHENA TRAITS:

Multitalented

Logical

Strategist

Practical

Confident

Gets the job done

A fighter

Intelligent

Crafty

Strong

Fighter for justice

HESTIA

Greek goddess of the hearth and temple

Wise woman who finds comfort in
solitude and keeping a home

HESTIA TRAITS:

Steady

Patient

Wise

Hearth-keeper

Inward focus on prayer and meditation

Inner-centeredness

A sense of wholeness

Illumination

Reflective

ISIS

The Egyptian heavenly queen

Mistress of life and health

Wife, mother and guardian of the family
and love relationships

ISIS TRAITS:

Mothering
Caregiver
Great healing power
Rebirth through love
Magical
Ability to breathe life into the weak and ailing

KUAN YIN

Chinese Buddhist goddess of
mercy and compassion

Compassion for oneself, others
and loved ones

KUAN YIN TRAITS:

Helper

Savior

Tender

Compassionate

Loves without judgment

Provider of health and long life

Comforter to those who are dying

Kindness and understanding at a soul level

LAKSHMI

The Hindu goddess of abundance,
luck, love and fertility

One of the most popular Hindu deities,
her auspicious nature and reputation for granting
fertility, luck, wealth and well-being seems to attract
devotees in almost every village in India.

LAKSHIMI TRAITS:

Prosperity, well-being
Royal power
Bountiful
Holy luster
Beauty
Abundant living
Happiness
Freedom from fear of poverty

BAST

Egyptian cat-headed goddess of play

BAST TRAITS:

Frolicker

Amusing

Pleasure

Joy

Music lover

Health and healing

Ruler of the moon and, of course, cats

Touched by a Goddess

For this exercise, think about what some of your ancient sisters would do in certain areas of your life. Feel free to include your favorite goddess. (See Modern-Day Goddess Books and Resources List for additional books about goddesses.) Below is an example of what happened when I tried this exercise.

Aphrodite, the goddess of love and beauty, inspired me to get a makeover at a makeup counter and read a book on love and romance. Artemis, the huntress and achiever, inspired me to go after a business project, and Athena's self-assurance helped me to feel calm during the meeting. After working hard, I renewed myself as Hestia would by going within with meditation. Next I frolicked on the beach to play as Bast would, and mothered myself with an aromatherapy bath as Isis might. Each night before I went to bed, I thought about how I could be more compassionate to myself and others like Kuan Yin. By the end of the week, my life felt enriched by focusing on these special goddess attributes.

Modern-Day Guiding Goddesses

Besides ancient goddesses, you can also create modern-day goddesses to help you. In the book *You Can Work Your Own Miracles* by internationally acclaimed author Napoleon Hill, (*Think and Grow Rich*), he talks about how he used unseen guides to help him succeed in life. While they are from his imagination, he calls them his "eight guiding princes" and treats them as "real people whose entire services are at his command throughout life." Hill's "unseen guides" are the princes of financial prosperity, sound physical health, peace of mind, hope, faith, love, romance and overall wisdom.

A modern-day goddess can also use the same principle to create her own support team for guidance. Here are my guiding goddesses, whom I can turn to or meditate to for wisdom. If I'm searching for a solution to a problem or looking for guidance or protection, I can ask myself what the Modern-Day Goddess of _____ would do or say in this situation.

> Modern-Day Goddess of Self-Love, Self-Esteem and Confidence (Remember to love yourself.)
>
> Modern-Day Goddess of Inner Wisdom (We can find a solution.)
>
> Modern-Day Goddess of Inner Peace (Meditate and breathe!)
>
> Modern-Day Goddess of Creativity (Let your imagination guide you.)
>
> Modern-Day Goddess of Good Health and Fitness (Just think how great you will feel afterwards.)
>
> Modern-Day Goddess of Fun, Laughter and Merriment (What would create fun and laughter in this moment?)
>
> Modern-Day Goddess of Miracles (Miracles can happen to you.)
>
> Modern-Day Goddess of Love and Romance (You deserve to be loved.)
>
> Modern-Day Goddess of Premenstrual Syndrome (Take away my cramps!)

Modern-Day Goddess of Sales (Find me what I want at 50 percent off.)

Modern-Day Goddess of Traffic (Clear up this traffic.)

Modern-Day Goddess of Parking Spaces (Find me a good space right in front where I don't have to parallel park.)

Modern-Day Goddess of Dates, Relationships, Husbands (Please, find me a great beloved.)

Modern-Day Goddess of Contests, Lottery (Please, let me win.)

Modern-Day Goddess of Finances (Please help me to have the courage and knowledge to be rich.)

Modern-Day Goddess of Emergencies and Miscellaneous (Please let me find my keys in the door, a good mechanic and enough money in my bank account to pay him.)

Inner-Wisdom Realization

You can draw on the traits of many ancient and modern-day goddesses for inspiration and strength.

Contemplations

1. Which ancient or modern-day guiding goddesses appeal to you? Why?
2. What could you do to invoke more of that goddess trait into your life?

3. Do you know a friend who has that trait who could inspire you?
4. If you were to make up your own goddess, who would she be?
5. Who do you think is a goddess in modern-day life? What traits does she have that you admire?

What I Learned

Women are amazing!
There is so much we can learn from our ancient sisters.
Every woman is a goddess.
Women rule!

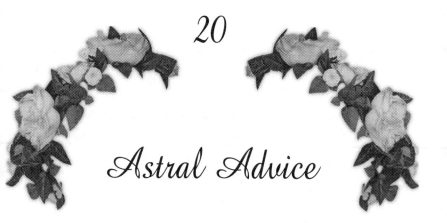

20

Astral Advice

Dear Diary:

Today, I cleaned out some old files when I found my astrology chart. It said I had so many houses located in different planets. I thought I could add to my resume that I was also into "astral real-estate development."

This made me think about all the astral advice I received during my life—some good and some bad.

Over the years, I've learned that all the answers we need are within us, and we have the free will to choose the way we want to approach life. So, when life gets challenging for a modern-day goddess, she must be careful not to give her power away by seeking too much information or inappropriate advice from an assortment of metaphysical consultants such as healers, tarot readers, astrologers, psychics and channelers instead of connecting with her inner wisdom. Otherwise, she may develop an AAA (astral advice addiction).

A wise girlfriend who is also a very practical personal coach, once said, "On the enlightenment path, you have to be careful not to become over-spiritualized and under-therapized." I agree. While it can be very inspiring and at times helpful to know what's in the stars, I've found its sometimes necessary to work with a good therapist to help you eliminate unempowering beliefs from your childhood that may be affecting your present life.

The first time I sought astral advice was when I was in my twenties, a bit naive and in the midst of an extremely stressful promotions job in the film industry. I was exhausted and looking for answers about my life. Each day I went to work on Fifth Avenue in New York City I would pass a sign that said: "Palm and psychic readings within—Madame Red Palm has the answers to all of your problems." At first I chuckled, but within a month, I decided to visit Madame on my lunch break. I thought, *Why not? It can't hurt.*

I should have known better. As I stepped into the tiny storefront, I heard Middle Eastern music playing in the background. I was immediately hit with a harsh scent of incense that irritated my senses and caused my stomach to flutter. (This, I have learned, is usually a warning sign or indigestion.) While intuition told me to leave, my curiosity wanted me to stay. Curiosity won. I slowly surveyed the room. Its contents consisted of frayed, red velvet curtains, a star-and-moon mobile, a worn-out armchair, a beaded doorway and a card table stacked with burning candles.

As I heard the beaded curtains sway, I turned toward the doorway to see Madame Red Palm entering the room. She was a short, heavy, dark-haired woman with intense eyes and thick black eyeliner that traveled back to her scalp. For twenty bucks, she would read your palm and face. "I am a third-generation Gypsy," Madame Red Palm explained. "Now let me take a look at you." She grabbed my palm and placed a long red fingernail on my skin. "Aaaha!" she said with delight. "I can see in your future that you will be successful in love, work, money and health." It sounded like a standard prediction, but I was glad not to hear any bad news. Just as I was about to ask her for specific details, a gray expression came over her face. "Ohhh, no. Ohhh, no," she said, looking me in the eyes. "I also see in your face that none of this will happen until you get rid of the curse that has been placed on you."

"A curse? Who placed a curse on me?" I asked in a surprised tone.

"I don't know. I just know it's there," she said with a grim face. "But I can remove it if you do two things," Madame Red Palm continued, as if she was an exterminator who had just discovered termites. "First, you must wear a packet of salt in your bra at all times to keep the bad energy away, and second, you must quickly bring me five hundred dollars or a new Kenmore refrigerator."

"A refrigerator, five hundred dollars?" I replied, aghast. Red Palm chose to ignore my outburst. "Yes, I need a new refrigerator, and I think a Kenmore in an avocado green would be nice."

I took this as a clear sign to exit. So I nodded my head,

paid her the twenty dollars and left as quickly as possible. I was relieved to be once again on Fifth Avenue, but I now felt even more uneasy about my life. I was so scared, I stopped off at a burger joint, grabbed a few packets of salt and discreetly went to the ladies room to affix them to my bra. I returned to the office with a scratchy sensation in my bosom that was with me throughout the day.

Madame Red Palm never saw me again. I often passed her shop, wondering if I would see a not-so-discerning client, wheeling in an avocado-colored Kenmore. Each time I thought of the dreaded curse, I would ask God to remove it from my mind and provide me with his guidance and protection. After a few days I stopped wearing the salt packets, when I realized how absurd the whole thing was. Plus, the temperature reached over 90 degrees, and I was beginning to feel like a French fry! I still don't know if wearing condiments helped, but one month later, the company I worked for declared bankruptcy—a life-changing event that caused me to reevaluate my life and begin a writing and comedy career.

After my Red Palm experience, I decided it was not wise to trust my soul to just anyone, whether they had a space on Fifth Avenue or a 900-psychic hotline. From that point on, I would only consider metaphysical consultants, healers and therapists that were referred. And even then I would use their services only on occasion after I spoke with them on the phone and my intuition gave me a confirmed yes.

Another problem that can occur when seeking guidance from others is that a modern-day goddess can also become confused if she receives advice from too many sources.

This happened to me while I was in the midst of rebuilding

my life after surgery. As an experiment, I decided to check in with as many consultants as I could find to see why it happened. (All through referrals, of course.) The answers I received about why the event occurred varied.

One astrologer said: "It was in the stars." A psychic: "It was in the air." A past-life therapist: "It was in your subconscious from a past life so you can resolve it in this life." A wise woman: "It was in your karma to be burned off." And my dentist: "It was in your teeth enamel. What about a whitening?"

When I was finished with my experiment, I was somewhat confused and overwhelmed, but with whiter teeth. I told the saga to my friend and the personal coach. She said: "Honey, you have TMI (Too Much Information)." She was right. So I sat down, meditated and asked myself the question why the accident had occurred. There were lots of answers: I needed to grow to another level spiritually, to discover I could rely on and love myself even through the worst of times. I needed to commit 100 percent to myself, to pursue my dreams and put my life back into balance.

Since my TMI adventure, I've learned to depend more on my own intuition. But during special times such as my birthday or the start of a new year, I like to have a session with a metaphysical consultant I've come to trust such as an astrologer. Before each session, I go within myself to see if the answers match. If I am in the midst of a life transition in any area, I also like to visit a good therapist and/or personal coach for extra support.

The good advisors which include a good therapist when needed have contributed to keeping me on track with my inner self, helping me see the lessons in the midst of turmoil, and have encouraged me to follow my dreams. There have been times when I've also received free divine messages from a book, a friend, a movie, a casual remark from a stranger and yes, even my mother.

It was a gifted, intuitive counselor who confirmed that a move to Santa Barbara from snowy Connecticut would be good for me (something I already felt). It was the same counselor who told me to forgive and let go of past hurts from my accident so I could experience all the gifts the universe wanted to offer me, including a soul mate. (I did, and he appeared.) It was another intuitive counselor who told me to try writing, since I had been a writer in a past life. Her words gave me the courage to just do it, even though I had doubts and poor grammar skills.

The Inner-Wisdom Meditation

Get comfortable in a chair or lie down on the floor. Have a journal or paper and pen nearby. Place one hand on your heart and the other on your stomach. Breathe. Visualize an all-knowing, wise, nurturing image of your higher power who has the answers to your question. See this as your highest self. Ask: What do I want right now? What do I need to know right know about a certain situation or my life in general? What action, if any, am I to take? What lesson am I to learn from this? Write down any insights in your journal and contemplate them. If an answer doesn't occur immediately, know that one may show up in the next few days through a friend, a book, a movie or an unexpected source.

It was a gifted astrologer who told me everything has a cycle, whether it's finances, love or career, and astrology can help pinpoint those cycles or one's life gifts. Her guidance helped me locate the perfect month to find a pre-owned dream car—a used, 1987 Mercedes, no less. It was a talented therapist who helped me sort out conflicting self-esteem messages so I could feel worthy of a good life, good work and a nice car! And a nurturing personal coach who taught me some practical tips to create a more balanced lifestyle. And it was God who delivered it all after I visualized and prayed for it to happen.

Regardless of who I consult with for advice, I always quiet myself with meditation and prayer, look within for my own answers, look for the lesson in any challenge, visualize my life the way I would like it to be, surrender everything to my higher power and ask for the divine plan of my life to manifest. I constantly work on believing that everything, even adversity, happens for the best. And when I look back on all the experiences of my life that made me the woman and modern-day goddess that I am, I can see that they did happen for the best.

Inner-Wisdom Realization

You have all the answers within you. And you can go inside throughout the day to ask God for guidance.

Modern-Day Goddess Contemplations

1. Have you ever received TMI (Too Much Information) or had a negative astral advice experience? What did you learn about yourself?
2. Have you ever worked with a gifted reader or a therapist—what did you learn?
3. Do you know how to go within to connect with your higher power and find the answer to any questions you may have? (See the Inner-Wisdom Meditation.)
4. Is there something from your past interfering with you moving forward in your present life?
5. How could talking to someone release anxiety and fear and improve your life?
6. Do you know any friends you could ask to refer you to someone qualified?

What I Learned

Rely on yourself first.
Stay away from TMI (Too Much Information).
Stay away from any Madame Red Palm sessions.

Always ask for referrals, and let your intuition guide you in your selection.

A good therapist and/or personal coach is a wise investment.

You Might Need Counseling If:

1. Your inner critic has a box seat in your head.
2. You are an adult and still upset over something your parents did thirty years ago.
3. You keep doing the same thing over and over again expecting a miracle.
4. Your friends have heard you complain about the same problem each week.
5. You keep dating the same kind of people, but only their names have changed.
6. Your idea of conflict management is leaving the scene of an argument.
7. Your idea of being assertive is sending your uncooked fish dinner back at a sushi restaurant.
8. You have a monthly $100 phone bill from calling the psychic 900 number hotline.
9. You are in the midst of a life transition that is causing you to lose sleep, such as getting married, relocating, starting your own business or ending yet another on-line relationship.
10. You keep denying you have an addiction to something like the Home Shopping Network even though your closets are packed with juicers, exercise equipment and cubic zirconia jewelry.

PART V:

Apply
Modern-Day
Goddess
Knowledge to
Your Life

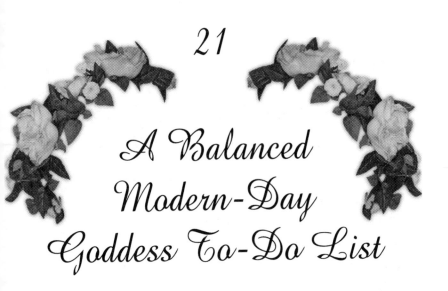

21

A Balanced Modern-Day Goddess To-Do List

Dear Diary:

Today it's becoming clear that if I want to continue on my path, I have to take the time to create balance in my life. A good friend of mine, who is a very balanced Libra, shared a secret with me on how to stay organized and in balance. It's a new twist on the old "things-to-do" list— a balanced modern-day goddess to-do list!

This is how it works. Instead of writing "meditate and take a walk" and then just below that "buy new tires and toilet paper," you lists things under different headings for the month. Then each week, I review my list and select priority items from each category. It's a great life balancing tool that helps me remain calm and balanced each day.

Here's a sample:

A Balanced Modern-Day Goddess To-Do List For the Month of _____

Relationship/Love
Plan a date night with my beloved
Mail out a card expressing my love
Meditate together
Take a sunset walk
Cook a meal together

Career
Write new chapters
Prepare for media interviews and telethon
Write speech for women's luncheon
Work on web site

Spirituality/Personal Growth
Meditate each day for at least twenty minutes
Visit meditation center on Monday nights
Read affirmations and write in journal daily
Self-nourish myself with an evening of reading by the fireplace

Family/Friends/Social
Mail card and gift for Mom's birthday
Arrange adult play-date with girlfriends
See new comedy film

Community/Contribution
Help out at church donation drive
Tithe to church and meditation center

Financial
Balance checkbook
Pay bills
Put money into savings

Health/Beauty/Fitness
Eat four servings of fruits and veggies each day
Schedule dentist appointment
Buy a new lipstick
Give myself a manicure
Go to the gym three times a week in morning
Attend yoga class on Wednesday
Take a bath with scented oils

Home
Food shopping
Buy flowers for altar
Do laundry

Miscellaneous
Return library books

Inner-Wisdom Realization

You can create wholeness in your life and eliminate unnecessary stress with a balanced to-do list.

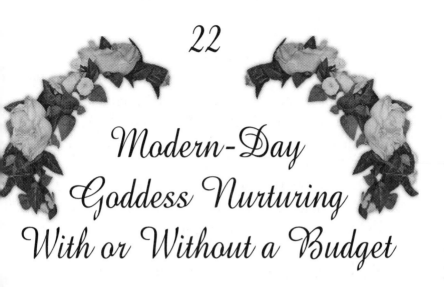

22

Modern-Day Goddess Nurturing With or Without a Budget

Dear Diary:

I just finished reading a great book <u>The Artist's Way,</u> by Julia Cameron. She said: "For every one good thing you do for yourself, God will do two." Now that's incentive to find ways to be self-nourishing.

One way to begin a self-kindness program is to establish a "self-nurturing fund" the same way you would a mutual fund where you contribute a little money to the account each month. Then you can use it to spend on you, guilt-free. But a modern-day goddess doesn't have to have a lot of money to nourish herself. Since I love a bargain just as much as anyone else, here are some ways to add more comfort, fun and joy into your life for little or no money.

Take an aromatherapy salt bath • read by the fireplace • walk by the beach • pick some fresh flowers • go to a farmer's market • play with your puppy • meditate on a mountaintop • meditate in a beautiful church • give yourself a beauty night with a manicure, pedicure and face mask • go to yard sales for treasures • check out consignment shops for clothes • have a clothes swapping party with your girlfriends • check out the designer sample sales and outlets • trade one professional skill for another, i.e., your marketing savvy or cooking skills for a session with a massage therapist • check out free fun events in your newspaper, like lectures and art openings • volunteer to usher for a play or an event you would like to attend • buy a two-for-one arts and entertainment ticket book • have a cup of tea at a four-star restaurant • spend a few hours in your favorite bookstore • go to the library and read all the great magazines • write a column for your local newspaper about something you love, i.e., restaurants, travel, film (it won't pay much, but you will be providing a service and have the opportunity to enjoy tickets to an event, a trip or restaurants you write about) • buy some beautiful votive candles, light them and say prayers of gratitude • watch great comedy films • dance in your living room to your favorite music.

Continue to save money in your self-nurturing fund, and when it comes time to "cash" in, think abundantly how you would like to spoil yourself. Here are some lavish examples.

Buy a year of monthly massages or facials
Take a trip you always wanted to take
Buy a fabulous outfit complete with shoes and accessories
Have fun making up your own list and enjoy!

Inner-Wisdom Realization

You are worthy of nurturing yourself on a consistent basis.

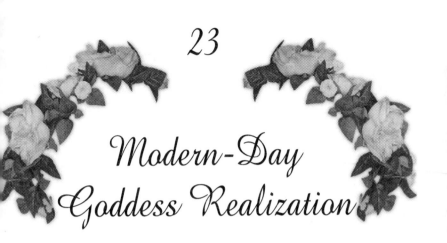

23

Modern-Day Goddess Realization

Dear Diary:

Today I gave myself the gift of sitting in the garden reflecting about my life. I took several moments to inhale the intoxicating scent of orange blossoms, listen to a whimsical hummingbird hum from plant to plant, and gaze at the majestic mountains against a crystal-blue sky. I felt so serene. Well, at least for five minutes—until I heard the garbage men arrive and compete in the trashcan Olympics. I waited until the garbage can games were over and quickly recentered myself with several more breaths until the games were eventually over.

As the gentle rays of sun filtered through the trees and a warm breeze touched my hair, I was overcome by how good I felt about myself and my now abundant life. I realized that by becoming a better person, I had created a better life.

So where do I go from here? Looking back, I can see that each of my en-lighten-up-ment explorations always brought me back to myself. And I plan to culti-vate all the things I've learned on my modern-day god-dess journey: lightheartedness, joy, a protection of grace, love, courage, self-nurturing, positive self-talk, medita-tion, yoga, inspiration from other goddesses and my never-ending curiosity about life.

While everyone has her own path, my wish is that by telling you my story, I have inspired and entertained you to explore your own divine inner-goddess self.

Photo by Jenna Hardesty.

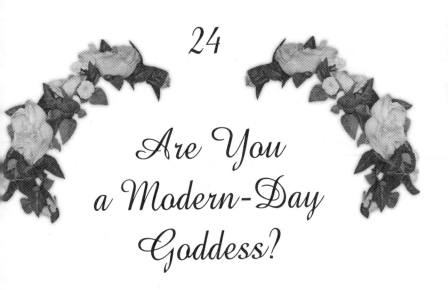

24

Are You a Modern-Day Goddess?

*N*ow that you've completed this book, are you a true modern-day goddess?

1. Do you have the urge to wear drapey, flowing clothes and floral headdresses?
2. Are you in touch with your inner spirit, inner soul and inner thighs?
3. Do you have a yoga instructor, acupuncturist, astrologer and Feng Shui consultant on speed dial?
4. Are you tofu tolerant?
5. Do you have a time-share in your local bookstore's self-help section?
6. Are most of your doctors from India?
7. Do you secretly desire your loved ones to address you as "my divine goddess"?

8. Have you paid money to learn how to sit still on a meditation pillow and be quiet?

9. Do you have an altar at home that consists of sacred items such as prayer requests, a picture of your guru, candles and a photo of Garth Brooks?

10. Are you married to or looking for a conscious male who is in touch with his inner guru?

11. Have you ever called in a Feng Shui consultant to rearrange your furniture, closet and love corner in order to manifest the perfect mate?

12. Do you talk to yourself in the form of affirmations such as, "I am a divine goddess, a child of God and a perfect size 5"?

13. Do think of Oprah as a higher power?

14. Is your soul delighted by beauty, the caress of grace and Godiva chocolates?

15. Do you get together with other goddesses for gatherings other than bridal showers, weddings and Tupperware parties?

16. Do you meditate instead of medicate?

17. Can you recognize a karmic, cosmic kick in the pants as God saying, "Yoo-hoo, wrong path, over here!"?

18. Are images from magazines glued to a life vision board that hangs on your wall your idea of art?

19. Do you practice Tantra sex as a conscious way to make love with your partner, instead of sex where you throw a tantrum if you don't have multiple orgasms?

20. Do you apologize after you've had a fight with your inner-self?

25

Become a Modern-Day Goddess: An Inspirational Blessing

Celebrate your feminine spirit, cultivate friendships with
glorious goddess girlfriends

Reach for joy, practice gratefulness

Nurture a cranky inner child, have
a love affair with yourself

Send yourself flowers, act surprised when they arrive

Trust your intuition, meditate, breathe

Be kind to your mind

Laugh each day, gaze at the stars, act on your dreams

Get in touch with your inner spirit,
inner soul, inner thighs!

Write in your journal, live an authentic life

Express your feelings, explore your creativity

Run with the wolves, swim with the dolphins,
play with the puppies

Delight in nature's beauty, her sunsets,
oceans and mountains

Take the road less traveled, but not when it's gridlocked

Pray for divine guidance, seek counsel from the wise

Practice creative fearlessness, watch for miracles

Stretch, exercise and love your body

Snuggle with your beloved or teddy bear

Make peace, make a difference, make love

Enjoy a sensuous bath, go to bed early

Dial your angels direct

An inspirational blessing.

Photo by Jenna Hardesty.

Modern-Day Goddess Communication

*S*ince it means a lot to me to know I made a difference in your life, I would be honored to hear about your enlightenment experiences as we travel together in modern-day goddess living. Please write or e-mail me with comments, topics you would like to see in my next book and any insights or stories you would like to share with me or future readers. Make sure to include your phone number, address and e-mail so I can contact you about the possibility of using your story in one of my next books. If your suggestion is used, you will receive credit.

Please visit my website at *www.moderndaygoddess.com* for information on workshops, public appearances, books, products and tapes and to be placed on a mailing list.

With love, joy and laughter.

Cynthia Daddona
Dharma • Karma Media Productions
1187 Coast Village Road #354
Santa Barbara, CA 93108
1-866-5DIVINE
E-mail: *cynthia@moderndaygoddess.com*
Web site: *www.moderndaygoddess.com*

About the Author

*C*ynthia Daddona is a dynamic on-air personality, inspirational speaker, journalist, humor writer and comedienne. As a multimedia goddess, Cynthia's work has appeared on "Access Hollywood," on CBS, E! Entertainment Television, USA Network, NPR radio and in *USA Today, The Los Angeles Times, First for Women, Men's Health* and *women.com*. She has interviewed over one hundred top celebrities and performed her humor at Caroline's, Stand-Up New York and special events. Cynthia has won numerous awards that include: a first-place excellence in writing award for her comedy scriptwriting at the Santa Barbara Writer's Conference, a recognition in the Inspirational category of the Writer's Digest Competition for an excerpt from her book *Diary of a Modern-Day Goddess*, and a "most innovative" award for her TV host/production work. A native of Connecticut, Cynthia currently lives in Santa Barbara, California, where she enjoys country living, goddess style.

Modern-Day Goddess Books and Resources

Introduction

Murdock, Maureen, *The Heroine's Journey Book* and workbook. Shambhala Publications, Boston, 1998 (*www.shambhala.com*).

Part I: Go West, Young Goddess A Very Moving Goddess

Boldt, Laurence G., *Zen and the Art of Making a Living: A Practical Guide to Creative Career Design*. Penguin, Arkana, New York, 1993.

Bolles, Richard Nelson, *What Color Is Your Parachute?* Ten Speed Press, Berkeley, California, 2000.

Cameron, Julia, *Vein of Gold: A Journey to Your Creative Heart*. A Jeremy Tarcher/Putnam Book, New York, 1996.

Canfield, Jack and Mark Victor Hansen, *The Aladdin Factor*. Berkley Books, New York, 1995.

Canfield, Jack, Mark Victor Hansen and Les Hewitt. *The Power of Focus*. Health Communications, Inc., Deerfield Beach, Florida, 2000.

Chopra, Deepak, *Seven Spiritual Laws to Success*. Amber-Allen Publishing, San Rafael, California, 1995.

Dyer, Wayne W., *Manifest Your Destiny—The Nine Spiritual Principles for Getting Everything You Want*. HarperCollins, New York, 1997.

Jeffers, Susan, Ph.D., *Feel the Fear and Do It Anyway*. Fawcett Columbine-Ballantine Books, New York, 1987.

Peale, Norman Vincent, *The Power of Positive Thinking*. Fawcett, New York, 1987.

McMakin, Jacqueline with Sonja Dyer, *Working From the Heart*. Harper San Francisco, 1993.

Sher, Barbara, *Live the Life You Love: In 10 Easy Steps*. Bantam, Doubleday, Dell Publishing, New York, 1997.

Tieger, Paul D., and Barbara Baron, *Do What You Are*. Little Brown & Co., New York, 1995.

The Lucky Break

Chopra, Deepak M.D., *How to Know God*. Harmony Books, New York, 2000.

Bloomfield, Harold M.D. with Phil Goldberg, *Making Peace with Your Past: The Six Essential Steps to Enjoying a Great Future*. HarperCollins, New York, 2000.

Daniel, Alma, Timothy Wyllie and Andrew Ramre, *Ask Your Angels*. Ballantine Books, New York, 1992.

Einstein, Patricia, *Intuition: The Path to Inner Wisdom*. Element Books, Boston, 2000.

Gurumayi Chidvilasananda, *Courage and Contentment: A Collection of Talks on Spiritual Life*, A Siddha Yoga Publication. SYDA Foundation, Fallsburg, New York, 1999.

Harvey, Andrew, *The Direct Path*. Broadway Books, New York, 2000.

Horn, Sam. *Concentrate: Get Focused and Pay Attention—When Life Is Filled with Pressures, Distractions and Multiple Priorities*. St. Martin's Press, New York, 2000.

James, Redfield, *The Celestine Prophecy*. Warner Books, New York, 1993.

————. *The Celestine Vision*. Warner Books, New York, 1997.

————. *The Tenth Insight and The Secret of Shambhala*. Warner Books, New York, 1999.

Kabat-Zinn, Jon, Ph.D., *Full Catastrophe Living: Using the Wisdom of Your Body and Mind to Face Stress, Pain and Illness*. Dell Publishing, New York, 1990.

Pine, Arthur with Julie Houston, *One Door Closes, Another Door Opens, Turning Your Setbacks into Comebacks*. Delacorte Press, New York, 1993.

Siegel, Bernie, *Love, Medicine and Miracles*. Harper & Row, New York, 1986.

————. *Peace, Love and Healing.* Harper & Row, New York, 1986.

Trungpa, Chogyam, *Shambhala—The Sacred Path of the Warrior.* Shambhala, Boston, 1995.

Virtue, Doreen Ph.D., *Divine Guidance.* Renaissance Books, Los Angeles, 1998.

Walsh, Neale Donald, *Conversations with God.* G.P. Putnam's Son's, New York, 1995.

————. *Meditations from Conversations with God, Book I.* Berkley Publishing Group, New York, 1997.

————. *Meditations from Conversations with God, Book II.* Hampton Road Publishing Co., Charlottsville, Virginia, 1997.

————. *Friendship with God. Random House,* New York, 1999.

Zukav, Gary, *The Seat of the Soul.* Fireside, New York, 1989.

————. *Soul Stories.* Simon & Schuster, New York, 1989.

Part II: The Modern-Day Goddess Basics Meditation 101

Transcendental Meditation

Benson, Herbert M.D., and Miriam Z. Klipper. *The Relaxation Response.* Morrow, Avon, New York, 2000.

Herbert Benson, M.D.
Mind/Body Medical Institute
New England Deaconness Hospital
110 Francis Street, Suite 1A
Boston, Massachusetts 02215

Borysenko, Joan, Ph.D., *Minding the Body, Mending the Mind* (Book), Bantam Books, New York, 1988.

Borysenko, Joan, *Beginner's Guide to Meditation* (Tape), *www.hayhouse.com.*

Joan Borysenko, Ph.D.
Mind/Body Health Services
393 Dixon Road
Boulder, Colorado 80302

Chopra, Deepak, M.D., *Ageless Body, Timeless Mind* (Book), Harmony Books, New York, 1993.

————. *Quantum Healing*. Bantam Books, New York, 1990.

————. *Perfect Health*. Harmony Books, New York, 1990.

————. *How to Know God*. Harmony Books, New York, 2000.

————. *Magical Mind, Magical Body* (Tape Series). Nightingale Conant, Niles, Illinois.

The Chopra Center for Well Being
7630 Fay Avenue
La Jolla, California 92037
www.chopra.com

Jack Kornfield Meditation for Beginners (Tape) *Sounds True*, *www.soundstrue.com*.
John Kabat-Zinn, Ph.D.
Stress Reduction and Relaxation Program
University of Massachusetts Medical Center
55 Lake Avenue North
Worcester, Massachusetts 01655-0267

New Dimensions Radio, *The Power of Meditation and Prayer*, Carlsbad, California, 1997.

Redfield, Salle Merrill, *The Joy of Meditation: A Beginner's Guide to Meditation* (Book and Tape) Warner Books, New York 1995.

Weil, Andrew, *Eight Weeks to Optimal Health*. Alfred A. Knopf, New York, 1997.

————. *Eight Meditations for Optimal Health*. (Tape) Upaya, 1997.

The SYDA Foundation and Bookstore
P.O. Box 600, 371 Brickman Road
South Fallsburg, New York 12779
www.siddhayog.org.

Siddha Yoga Meditation Audiotapes

Chidvilasananda, Gurumayi, *Meditation Instructions*, Volume One, SYDA Foundation, Fallsburg, New York, 1998.

Om Namah Shivaya—Bhupali Raga—("slow, majestic, evoking deep contentment")

Om Namah Shivaya—Shiva Bhaira Raga—("slow, tender, evoking the mystery of the divine")

Om Namah Shivaya—The King of Mantras—(upbeat version)

Pasayadan and Mahalakshmi Stotram, as sung in Siddha Yoga Meditation Ashrams

Books

Chidvilasananda, Gurumayi, *The Yoga of Discipline*. SYDA Foundation, Fallsburg, New York, 1996.

———. *Enthusiasm*. SYDA Foundation, Fallsburg, New York, 1997.

Swami Muktananda, *Meditate: Happiness Lies Within You, A Siddha Yoga Publication*. SYDA Foundation, Fallsburg, New York, 1999.

———. *Mystery of the Mind*. SYDA Foundation, Fallsburg, New York, 1992.

Spring Hill Music

a division of Spring Hill Media Group

P.O. Box 800

Boulder, Colorado 80306

springhillmedia.com

Anand, Margot, Everyday Ecstasy: *Music for Passion, Spirit & Joy*. Spring Hill Music, Boulder, Colorado, 1998.

Robert Gass with Kathleen Brehany Chanting: *Discovery Spirit in Sound*. Broadway Books, New York, 2000.

Gass, Robert and On Wings of Song, OmNamah Shivaya—10th anniversary deluxe edition (Tape) (cited by *New Age Journal* as one of the twenty most influential recordings of the past 20 years)

Gass, Robert and On Wings of Song, Enchanted (Tape) A collection of chants from Pachelbel's Canon to Om Namah Shivaya to Alleluia.

———. Chant: *Spirit in Sound, The Best of World Chant*.

Krishna Das, Pilgrim Heart (Tape) Troika Records, New York, 1998.

Web sites of other places to check out soothing music:

www.windhamhill.com

(featuring artists such as George Winston and Jim Brickman)

www.hayhouse.com

www.naranda.com

Music and Healing

Don Campbell, *The Mozart Effect* (Book), Avon Books, New York, 1997.

———. *Volume 1 Strengthen the Mind*, Volume 2: *Heal the Body*, Volume 2: *Unlock the Creative Spirit* (tapes) *www. springhillmedia.com*.

Hay House, Inc.,
P.O. Box 5100, Carlsbad
California 92018-5100
www.hayhouse.com
Sound Choices for Healing, Home, Relaxation, Children and Work

Sound Covenant: The Blessing of Music, A ministry for music and healing *info@soundcovenant.org.*

Maria Del Rey's Lullabies of Latin America (Grammy-nominated). Nurturing music for the whole family.

Laughter

Cousins, Norman. *Anatomy of an Illness as Perceived by the Patient.* Norton, New York, Norton, 1979.

Goodheart, Annette Ph.D., *Laughter Therapy: How to Laugh About Everything in Your Life That Isn't Really Funny.* California, 1994.

Klein, Allen, *The Healing Power of Humor.* J.P. Tarcher, Los Angeles, 1989.

LaRoche, Loretta, *RELAX–You May Only Have a Few Minutes Left.* Villard, New York, 1998.

The Humor Potential, Inc.
20 North Street
Plymouth, Massachusetts 02360
www.stressed.com

Goodman, Joel, *Laffirmations: 1,001 Ways to Add Humor to Your Life and Work.* Health Communications, Deerfield Beach, Florida, 1995.

Dr. Joel Goodman, Director
The Humor Project, Inc.
480 Broadway, Suite 210
Saratoga, New York 12866-2288
website: *www.humorproject.com*
International Humor Conference, Books,
Speakers Bureau and Magazine.

Sark, *Living Juicy.* Celestial Arts, Berkeley, California, 1994.

Comedy Performing and Writing

Perrett, Gene, *Successful Stand-Up Comedy.* Samuel French, Hollywood, California, 1994.

Perrett, Gene, Martha Bolton, *Talk About Hope—Two Bob Hope Writers Trade Stories.* Jester Press, Little Falls, Minnesota, 1998.

Carter, Judy, *Stand-Up Comedy: The Book*. Dell, New York, 1989.

Vorhaus, John, *The Comic Toolbook—How To Be Funny Even If You're Not*. Silman-James Press, Los Angeles, 1994.

Writing

Godlberg, Natalie, *Writing Down to the Bones*. Shambhala Publications, Boston, 1986.

Perrett, Gene, *Become a Richer Writer*. Jester Press, Little Falls, Minnesota, 1998.

Poynter, Dan, *Write and Grow Rich*. Para Publishing, Santa Barbara, California, 1999.

Provost, Gary, *100 Ways to Improve Your Writing*. NAL, Penguin, Putnam, Inc. New York, 1985.

Journaling

Cameron, Julia, *The Artist's Way: A Spiritual Path to Higher Creativity*. Putnam Publishing, New York, 1992.

Offner, Rose, *Journal to the Soul*. Gibbs-Smith Publishing, Salt Lake City, Utah, 1997.

Offner, Rose, *Journal to Intimacy, A Couple's Journal for Sustaining Love*. Celestial Arts, Berkeley, California, 2000.

Riner, Tristine, *The New Diary, How to Use a Journal for Self-Guidance and Creativity*. Putnam Publishing, New York, 1979.

Segalove, Ilena, *A Journal For All Your Feelings, Frenzies, Rants and Celebrations*. Andrews McMeel, Kansas City, 2000.

Comedy/Humor

Allen, Steve, *How to Be Funny*. McGraw-Hill, New York, 1987.

Ball, Lucille, *The Best of Old Time Radio*, audiotapes (Radio Spirits) *www.mediabay.com*

The Best of Erma Bombeck. Andrews & McMeel, Kansas City, 1997.

Bhaerman, Steve, Swami Beyondananda, *Duck Soup for the Soul—The Way of Living Louder and Laughing Longer*. Sourcebooks, Inc., Naperville, Illinois 2000.

———. *Driving Your Own Karma*. Destiny Books, Inner Traditions, Rochester, Vermont, 1989.

———. *Live Concert Audio Tapes, Yogi from Muskogee, Enlightening Strikes Again, Don't Squeeze the Shaman*. Lite Headed Productions at *www.beyondanada.com*.

Bombeck, Erma, *Forever, Erma, Best-Loved Writing from America's Favorite Humorist*. Andrews McMeel, Kansas City, 1996.

Burns, George, *Dr. Burns Prescription for Happiness*. G.P. Putnams Sons, New York, 1984.

Writings, Books, Tapes, TV or Movies By:

Lucille Ball

Dave Barry

Albert Brooks

Mel Brooks

Erma Bombeck

Elayne Boosler

Carol Burnett

George Burns and Gracie Allen

Bill Cosby

Stan Freburg

Whoopi Goldberg

Goldie Hawn

Bob Hope

Steve Martin

Bette Midler

Paula Poundstone

Carl Reiner

Paul Reiser

Gary Shandling

Lily Tomlin

Robin Williams

Jonathan Winters

Steven Wright

Comedy Videos to Rent for Some Laughs

Get Bruce!

Keeping the Faith

L.A. Story

Living Out Loud

Private Benjamin

Runaway Bride

When Harry Met Sally

Comedy Collections

But Seriously . . . The American Comedy Box: The Most Comprehensive Collection of Recorded Comedy from 1915–1994. Rhino.

The Comic Relief Series

Rhino Records

10635 Santa Monica Blvd.

Los Angeles, California 90025-4900

www.rhino.com

Goddess Self-Talk

Carey, Baker, *Prosperity Aerobics*. Heaven on Earth Publishing, Woodstock, New York, 1995.

Carnegie, Dale, *How to Stop Worrying and Start Living*. Pocket Books, New York, 1948.

Hay, Louise L., *You Can Heal Your Life*. Hay House, Carlsbad, California, 1987.

———. *Empowering Woman*, 1997.

McWilliams, Peter, *You Can't Afford the Luxury of a Negative Thought.* Prelude Press, Los Angeles, 1995.

Shad, Helmstetter, *What to Say When You Talk to Yourself.* Pocket Books, New York, 1982.

Yogacize
Iyengar, B.K.S., *Light on Yoga* (Book). Schocken Books, New York, 1977.

Videos
Friend, John, *Yoga: Alignment and Form and Yoga for Meditators.* SYDA Foundation. *www.bookstore.siddhayoga.org*

Yee, Rodney, *Power Strength Yoga for Beginners with Rodney Yee* *www.living arts.com.*

———. *Yoga for Two—Beginners www.livingarts.com*

Modern-Day Goddess Shopping
Blanchard, Ken, *Big Bucks and Personal Finance.* Morrow-Avon, New York, 2000.

———. *Three Keys to Empowerment.* Berrett-Koehler Publishers, San Francisco, 1999.

Chopra, Deepak, M.D., *Creating Affluence.* New World Library, Novato, California, 1993.

Giles, Gerry, *Moneylove.* Warner Books, New York, 1978.

Gaines, Edwene, *Prosperity Plus!* and *Riches and Honor!* Audiotapes

Edwene Gaines Seminars

The Prosperity Products/The Masters' School

P.O. Box 294

Mentone, Alabama 35984

www.prosperityproducts.com

Hill, Napoleon, *Think and Grow Rich.* Fawcett Books New York, 1987.

———. *The Master Key to Riches, Succeed and Grow Rich Through Persuasion,* New American Library, New York, 1989.

———. *Grow Rich! With Peace of Mind,* Fawcett Books, New York, 1986.

———. *Think and Grow Rich: A Black Choice* with Dennis Kimbro. Fawcett Books, New York, 1996.

Kiyosaki, Robert, *Rich Dad, Poor Dad,* Warner Books, New York, 2000.

Orman, Suze, *Nine Steps to Financial Freedom.* Crown Publishing, New York, 1997.

———. *The Courage to Be Rich.* Putnam Publishing, New York, 1999.

Ponder, Catherine, *The Prosperity Secrets of the Ages*. DeVorss, Marina del Rey, California, 1986.

———. *Open Your Mind to Prosperity*, 1971.

———. *The Dynamic Laws of Prosperity*, 1962.

———. *Dare to Prosper*, 1983.

———. *The Prospering Power of Love*, 1996.

Walker, Elizabeth, *The Abundant Woman*. Belgrave House, San Francisco, 1998.

Glorious Goddess Girlfriends

Berry, Carmen Renee and Tamara Traeder, *Girlfriends*. Wildcat Canyon Press, a division of Circulus Publishing Group, Inc., Berkeley, California, 1995.

———. *Girlfriends for Life*. Wildcat Canyon Press, Berkeley, California, 1999.

———. *Girlfriend Gift:Reflections on the Extraordinary Bonds of Friendship*. Wildcat Canyon Press, Berkeley, California, 2000.

Engel, Beverly, *Women Circling the Earth—A Guide to Fostering Community, Healing and Empowerment*. Health Communications, Inc., Deerfield Beach, Florida, 2000. *www.hci-online.com*.

Ornish, Dean, M.D., *Love and Survival*. HarperPerennial, New York, 1998.

Rubin, Lillian B., *Just Friends: The Role of Friendship in Our Lives*. HarperCollins, New York, 1985.

Part III: *Modern-Day Goddess Love*

Italians

Buscaglia, Leo, *Loving Each Other*. Simon & Schuster, New York, 1995.

———. *Love*. Harcourt Brace College Publisher, Fort Worth, Texas, 1995.

Loren, Sophia, *Sophia Loren's Recipes and Memories*. GT Publishing Corp., New York, 1998.

Mayes, Frances, *Under a Tuscan Sun*. Chronicle Books, San Francisco, 1996.

———. *Bella Tuscany*, Broadway Books, New York, 1999.

Goddess Self-Love: Dating Yourself

Shakti, Gawain, *Creative Visualization*. Bantam, New York, 1982.

————. *Living in the Light*. New World Library, Novato, California, 1998.

————. *True Prosperity*. New World Library, Novato, California 1997.

Modern-Day Goddess Love Letter

Hay, Louise L., *You Can Heal Your Life*, Hay House, Carlsbad, California, 1987.

————. *Loving Thoughts for Loving Yourself,* Hay House, Carlsbad, California, 1993.

Hay, Louise and Friends, *Gratitude: A Way of Life*, Hay House, Carlsbad, California, 1996.

Conscious Male Wanted

Johnson, Robert, *He: Understanding Masculine Psychology*, Perennial Library, New York, 1989.

————. *She: Understanding Feminine Psychology*, HarperCollins, New York, 1989.

————. *We: Understanding the Psychology of Romantic Love*, Harper San Francisco, 1995.

Miller, Carolyn, *Soulmates: Following Inner Guidance to the Relationship of Your Dreams*. H.J. Kramer, Inc., Tiburon, California, 2000.

Moore, Thomas, *Soulmates*. HarperCollins, New York, 1996.

Divine Dating

Kast, Charlotte, Ph.D., *If the Buddha Dated: A Handbook for Finding Love on the Spiritual Path*. Penguin Group, New York, 1999.

Romantic Spiritual Videos to Rent

City of Angels
Made in Heaven

Romantic Spiritual Comedy

Defending Your Life
Keeping the Faith

Williamson, David, D. Unity Church Minister, Gay Lynn Williamson, M.A. Psy., and Robert Knapp, M.D. *Twelve Powers in You (Based on the 12 powers pioneered by Charles Fillmore)*. Health Communications, Inc., Deerfield Beach, Florida, 2000. *www.hci-online.com* and *www.12powers2000.org*.

Unity Village
1901 NW Blue Parkway
Unity Village, MO 64065-0001

The Daily Word, an inspirational monthly affirmations booklet and information about a Unity Church near you.

Love Modern-Day Goddess Style

Anand, Margo, *The Art of Sexual Ecstasy.* Jeremy P. Tarcher/Putnam, New York, 1989.

Barnett, Doyle, *Twenty Communication Tips for Couples.* New World Library, Novato, California, 1995.

————. *Twenty Advanced Communication Tips for Couples.* Crown Publishing Group, New York, 1997.

Carlson, Richard Ph.D., and Kristine, *Don't Sweat the Small Stuff in Love.* Hyperion, New York, 1999.

Carter-Scott, Cherie, *If Love Is a Game, These Are the Rules.* Broadway Books, New York, 1998.

Chapman, Gary, *The Five Love Languages: How to Express Heartfelt Commitment to Your Mate.* Northfield Publishing, Chicago, 1995 (book and tape).

Chidvilasananda, Gurumayi, *The Magic of the Heart—Reflections on Divine Love.* SYDA Foundation, Fallsburg, New York, 1996.

De Angelis, Barbara, Ph.D., *Are You the One for Me?* Dell Trade, New York, 1992.

————. *Real Moments.* Dell, New York, 1994.

————. *Secrets About Life Every Woman Should Know.* Hyperion, New York, 1999.

Fowler, Beth, *Could You Love Me Like My Cat.* Fireside, New York, 1996.

Godek, Gregory, J. P., *1,001 Ways to Be Romantic.* Sourcebooks, Naperville, Illinois, 1995.

Gray, John, Ph.D., *Men Are from Mars, Women Are from Venus* series. HarperCollins, New York, 1992.

————. *How to Get What You Want and Want What You Get.* HarperCollins, New York, 1999.

Harville, Hendrix, Ph.D., *Getting the Love You Want.* Harper Perennial, New York, 1998.

Hendricks, Gay and Kathlyn Ph.D., *Conscious Loving,* Bantam, New York, 1990.

————. *The Conscious Heart,* Bantam, 1997.

Hendricks, Gay, *The Ten-Second Miracle*. Harper San Francisco, 1998.

Jampolsky, Gerald G., *Love Is Letting Go of Fear*. Celestial Arts, Berkeley, California, 1979.

Keyes, Ken Jr. *The Power of Unconditional Love*. Love Line Books, Coos Bay, Oregon, 1990.

Kroeger, Otto and Janet M. Thuesen, *Sixteen Ways to Love Your Lover, Understanding Personality Types*. Tilden Press, New York, 1999.

Mandel, Bob, *Heart Over Heels—50 Ways Not to Lose Your Lover*. Celestial Arts, Berkeley, California, 1989.

———. *Open Heart Therapy*. Celestial Arts Publishing Co., Berkeley, California, 1995.

Muir, Charles and Caroline *Tantra: Art of Conscious Loving*. Mercury House, San Francisco, California, 1989.

Offner, Rose, *Journal to Intimacy, A Couples' Journal for Sustaining Love*. Celestial Arts, Berkeley, California, 2000.

———. *The Lover's Bedside Companion*. Casablanca Press, Weymouth, Massachusetts, 1994.

Ponder, Catherine, *The Prospering Power of Love*. DeVorss Publishing, Marina del Rey, California, 1996.

Ruiz, Don Miguel, *The Mastery of Love: A Practical Guide to the Art of Relationship*. Amber-Allen Publishing, San Rafael, California, 1999.

Aron, Elaine, N., Ph.D., *The Highly Sensitive Person in Love*. Broadway Books, New York, 2000.

Vissell, Joyce and Barry, *The Heart's Wisdom*. Conari Press, Berkeley, California, 1999.

A Chakra-Balancing Massage

Diemer, Deedre, M.A., C.H.T., *The ABC's of Chakra Therapy—A Workbook*. Samuel Weiser, Inc., York Beach, Maine, 1998.

Virtue, Doreen, Ph.D., *Chakra Clearing, Awakening Your Healing Power*. audiocassette *hayhouse.com*.

Simpson, Liz, *The Book of Chakra Healing*. Sterling Publishing Company, New York, 1999.

Feng Shui Fun

Collins, Terah Kathryn, *Home Design with Feng Shui*. Hay House, Carlsbad, California, 1999.

———. *The Western Guide to Feng Shui, Room by Room*. Hay House, Carlsbad, California, 1999.

Rauch Carter, Karen, *Move Your Stuff, Change Your Life: How to Use Feng Shui to Get Love, Money, Respect and Happiness*. Fireside, New York, 2000.

Too, Lilian, *The Complete Illustrated Guide to Feng Shui*. Element Books, Rockport, Maine, 1996.

Inspiring Ancient Goddess and Modern-Day Guiding Goddesses

Bolen M.D., Jean Shinoda, *Goddesses in Every Woman*. Harper Perennial, New York, 1984. From the Opening Summary page "Who Are The Goddesses?" and pages 49, 75, 80, 111, 113, 239, 241.

Kinsley, David, *The Goddesses' Mirror: Visions of the Divine from East and West*. State University Press of New York, Albany, 1989. p.35, 37, 41, 53, 55, 139, 169, 173.

Marashinsky, Amy, *The Goddess Oracle*. Illustrated by Hran Janto. Element Books, Boston, 1997. p. 31, 32, 89, 98.

Parkhurst, Juni, *The Goddess Card Pack*. Sterling Publishing, New York, 1999. p. 40, 46, 54, 55, 68, 84.

Other Items and Books of Interest

Blair, Nancy, *Amulets of the Goddess*. Wingbow Press, Oakland, California, 1993.

Keating, Father Thomas, *Open Mind, Open Heart*. Continuum International Publishing, 1993.

Leon, Vicki, *Uppity Women* (Book Series) *of Ancient Times, Renaissance, Medieval and Shakespearean Times*. Conari Press, Berkeley, California.

Martin, Katherine, *Women of Courage, Inspiring Stories from the Women Who Lived Them*. New World Library, Novato, California 1999.

Monaghan, Patricia, *The Goddess Companion*. Llewellyn Publications, St. Paul, Minnesota, 2000.

Napoleon, Hill, *You Can Work Your Own Miracles*. Fawcett Gold Medal, New York, 1971.

Stasinopoulos, Agapi, *Conversations with the Goddesses*. Stewart, Tabori & Chang, New York, 1999.

Astral Advice

Borysenko, Joan, *A Woman's Book of Life: The Biology, Psychology and Spirituality of the Feminine Life Cycle*. Berkley Publication Group, New York, 1998.

Chopra, Deepak M.D., *How to Know God*. Harmony Books, New York, 2000.

Eichenbaum, Diane, *Soul Signs*. Simon & Schuster, New York, 1998.

MacLaine, Shirley, *Going Within*. Bantam, New York, 1990.

Virtue, Doreen, Ph.D., *Divine Guidance*. Renaissance Books, Los Angeles, 1998.

A Balanced Goddess To-Do List

Covey, Stephen, *The Seven Habits of Highly Effective People*. Firestone, New York, 1990.

Davidson, Jeff, MBA, CMC, *The Idiots Guide to Managing Your Time*. Alpha Books, MacMillan, New York, 1999.

Lockwood, Georgene, *The Idiot's Guide to Organizing Your Life*. Alpha Books, MacMillan, New York, 1999.

Modern-Day Goddess Nurturing With or Without a Budget

Harris, Rachel, *Twenty Minute Retreats: Revive Your Spirit in Just Minutes a Day with Simple Self-Led Exercises*. Henry Holt & Co, New York, 2000.

Louden, Jennifer, *The Woman's Comfort Book*, Harper, San Francisco, 1992.

————. *The Comfort Queen's Guide to Life: Creating All That You Need with Just What You've Got*. Harmony Books, New York, 2000.

————. *The Woman's Retreat Book*. Harper, San Francisco, 1999.

Other Books of Interest

Ban, Sarah, Breathnach, *Simple Abundance*. Warner Books, New York, 1995.

Phelps, Stanlee and Nancy Austin, *The Assertive Woman*. Impact Publishers, Atascadero, California, 3rd edition 1997.

St. James, Elaine, *Inner Simplicity*. Andrews McMeel, Kansas City, 2000.

————. *Simplify Your Life*. Hyperion, New York, 1994.

————. *365 Simple Reminders to Keep Life Simple*. Andrews McMeel, Kansas City, 2000.

Ruiz, Don Miguel, *The Four Agreements: A Practical Guide to Personal Freedom*. Amber-Allen Publishing, San Rafael, California, 1997.

The Breath of Spirit

The Giuliana Legacy
By Alexis Masters

This exquisite book traces the heroine's discovery of her family's mystic and healing traditions. You will be enthralled as you follow her on a quest to save her ancestors' ancient spiritual tradition from extinction. A truly mesmerizing and timeless story of love and redemption!

Code #7850 • Quality Paperback • $14.95

One Last Hug Before I Go
By Carla Wills-Brandon

This groundbreaking book explores the universal phenomenon of the deathbed vision. The shared visions and experiences provide understanding, empathy and comfort for those left behind. Along with a better insight into the death process, you will come to see it as a spiritual adventure, not a tragic and fearful ending to life.

Code #7796 • Quality Paperback • $12.95

Quiet your Mind

Code #8385 • Quality Paperback • $8.95

Eternal Blessings

Blessings are simple yet heartfelt messages that you can bestow on the people you care about, whether you want to remind your spouse of your love, cheer up a coworker who's having a bad day, or comfort a friend facing a trying time you'll find the perfect words in this little gem.

Practical Meditation

A peaceful volume that provides a compilation of inspirational passages, exercises and mantras that, when practiced over time, will bring you a sense of clarity, self-awareness and peace of mind.

Code #827X • Quality Paperback • $10.95

New Soup for the Whole Family

Chicken Soup for Little Souls
Code #8121• Quality Paperback • $12.95

**Chicken Soup for the
Preteen Soul**
Code #8008 • Quality Paperback • $12.95

**Chicken Soup for the
Expectant Mother's Soul**
Code #7966 • Quality Paperback • $12.95

**Chicken Soup for the
Parent's Soul**
Code #7478• Quality Paperback • $12.95

Selected titles are also available in hardcover, audiocassette and CD.

Available wherever books are sold.
To order direct: Phone — **800.441.5569** • Online — **www.hci-online.com**
Prices do not include shipping and handling. Your response code is **BKS**.